Planted in the House of the Lord:

God, Israel, and the Church

Joseph Shulam

Planted in the House of the Lord:

God, Israel, and the Church

Joseph Shulam

Netivyah Bible Instruction Ministry

2011

Netivyah Bible Instruction Ministry
P.O.B. 8043
Jerusalem, 91080
Israel

netivyah@netivyah.org.il
www.netivyah.org

ISBN (978-0-9818730-7-7)

Planted in the House of the Lord:
God, Israel, and the Church

Joseph Shulam

Edited by Elizabeth Wakefield

Cover painting by Erin Zofef

Printed in Israel 2011

To my children Barry and Danah

Contents

Introduction

When visiting the sites of the ancient world in the Middle East, Turkey, and Greece, one can see magnificent marble temples dedicated to pagan gods such as Athena, Zeus, Poseidon, Vulcan, and many others. In the area of ancient Persia, stands the *Persepolis* with many huge, fabulous buildings. Egypt also still has temples built in the Fifteenth or even the Eighteenth century BCE that make modern buildings look like shacks. They have pillars six feet in diameter made of marble and red granite in Aswan that have been standing for 3,500 years. The beauty, ceremony, and order of these temples as well as the beautiful silk clothing that the priests wore are all very impressive, yet the undeniable truth is that all these temples were made for idols.

Most people in the Western world are theoretically so acclimated to the idea of monotheism that they have no idea what idolatry is or what is wrong with it. The Word of God refers to Gentile idolatry as "darkness," and it truly is dark, as anyone who has ever witnessed it firsthand can attest. Those who worship idols are absolutely enslaved to darkness. They are enslaved to pleasing competing divine figures, each with their own whims and differing expectations. Today one can travel to countries like Japan and Taiwan and experience the astounding contradiction between the external modernity of people's technologically driven lives and the internal weight of fear and slavery that comes from the practice of idolatry. They spend their fortunes trying to appease their dead ancestors by burning ghost money or buying food offerings.

They struggle to appease and avoid curses laid upon them by various gods they failed to satisfy. People literally murder and commit suicide because of their enslavement to pagan gods. Satan uses idolatry to achieve these tragic results because his ultimate goal is to destroy all life due to his hatred of the Creator. Despite all our modern technology and humanitarian "advancements," most of humanity is still enslaved to Satan's deception through the darkness of idolatry.

Part of the mission of the Jewish people is to spread the light of the knowledge of the One God throughout the entire earth in order to overcome this darkness. This is what it means to be "a light to the nations." When Yeshua came to earth as the Messiah, his disciples spread the Gospel and the light of monotheism all throughout the known world, proving that He was a "light to the world" and not just to the Jewish people. Unfortunately, much of the non-Jewish world quickly forgot the basic principles of monotheism that the disciples taught them and syncretized their idolatrous past into their belief in Yeshua and the God of Israel. Their misunderstanding of the nature of Yeshua and the God of Israel created a Trinity rooted in paganism instead of a Trinity rooted in monotheism and the truth of the Bible. Of course, these matters are not simple to understand, but we must return to a more accurate comprehension of the nature of God if we want to serve Him better as his messengers in our dark world. Although the One God whom we know through the Scriptures is impossible to grasp and understand with mere human reasoning, He has revealed Himself to us in his creation, in humanity, and in history. The God of Israel chose to make his first earthly dwelling place in a tent in the heart of the desert in order to eventually be able to dwell in every human heart.

The God of the Bible may seem to us to be more absent than He was in the days of the Bible. We may find it hard to see his work in our everyday lives and in ordinary people. Nevertheless, He is still greatly concerned with his creation, especially with his people. After two thousand years of conflicts in Jewish-Christian history, however, there are many Jews and Christians who are confused about who composes God's people and who God really is.

The study of the theology of the Church is called Ecclesiology, which comes from the Greek word *ekklesia*, which means "assembly" or "gathering." Ecclesiology is greatly concerned with the relationship between God and his people and the identity of those people. Even a quick perusal of the Old Testament makes it very clear that God chose Israel, the physical descendants of Abraham, Isaac, and Jacob to be a special group of people belonging to Him. Many Christians become confused, however, when they see in the New Testament that Jesus, the Jewish Messiah, was not accepted by the majority of the Jewish people. The Apostles and the Church's earliest members were all Jewish, but the Church became increasingly less Jewish as the message of Yeshua spread rapidly across the Greco-Roman world. The Church forgot its roots and denied the special relationship between God and the Jewish people. Today there is a lot of confusion in the Church about her identity and the relationship between her Jewish and non-Jewish members as well as confusion about the relationship she should have with the main body of the Jewish people who do not believe in Yeshua. The Apostle Paul wrote a great deal about this subject, but unfortunately historical Church leaders have largely misunderstood him and have used their misinterpretations to commit many crimes against the Jewish people. It is the goal of this book to clarify this important subject of the identity of and the relationship between God, Israel, and the Church.

Ephesians 2:11-22 is a key passage for understanding the basics of Ecclesiology. Here Paul draws a metaphor of the Church as a structure composed of three separate but connected parts: God, Israel, and the Church. Many of the incorrect understandings of Ecclesiology come from misinterpretations of this passage, which says, *"Therefore, remember that formerly you who are Gentiles by birth, who are called 'uncircumcised' by those who call themselves 'the circumcision' (that done in the body by the hands of men)— remember that at that time you were separate from Messiah, excluded from citizenship in Israel and foreigners to the covenants of the promise, without hope and without God in the world. But now in the Messiah Jesus you who were once far away have been brought near through the blood of the Messiah. For He Himself is our peace, who has made the two one and has destroyed the barrier of the dividing wall, by abolishing in His flesh the enmity, the Law of commandments and regulations that He might make the two into one new man, thus establishing peace and might reconcile then both in one body to God through the cross, by having put to death the enmity. He came and preached peace to you who were far away and peace to those who were near. For through Him we both have access to the Father by one Spirit. So then you are no longer strangers and aliens, but fellow citizens with the saints and members of God's household, built upon the foundation of the apostles and prophets, with the Messiah Jesus Himself as the chief cornerstone. In Him the whole building is joined together and rises to become a holy temple in the Lord. And in Him you too are being built together to become a dwelling of God in the Spirit."*

The title for this book comes from Psalm 92:12-15, which says, *"The righteous flourish like the palm tree and grow like a cedar in Lebanon. They are planted in the house of the Lord; they flourish in the courts of our God. They still bear fruit in old age; they are ever full of sap and green to declare that the Lord is upright. He is my rock, and there is no unrighteousness in him."* It is God's desire for his people to be like flourishing greenery, the very picture of spiritual health in the desert wilderness of idolatry and hopelessness that fills the world. When He chose Israel, He planted them in his heavenly Temple forever as the pillar of his plan to redeem the whole world. Likewise, those from among the nations who have been grafted in to the olive tree of Israel through their belief in and following after Yeshua, the Messiah of Israel, also have a firmly rooted foundation in the house of God. These branches are dependant upon their roots and their heavenly Gardener if they are to continue to be strong and healthy. Too many people today fail to understand how they are planted in the House of the Lord, who planted them there, and what kind of tree they are even supposed to be. Because of this confusion, they are cut off from their roots, and their faith withers away in the storms and droughts of life

The foundation for accurate and enduring Ecclesiology and spiritual identity is a triangle composed of three interconnected parts: God, Israel, and the Church. Without any one of these three elements, the whole structure collapses. Without a proper understanding of each element, the building will be warped and twisted. Therefore, this book will examine each of these three elements individually to try to discern what their relationship is to one another. Once these elements are understood properly, the Church will be more able to stand firm as a haven of refuge and a beautiful temple of the Living God in this troubled world until the return of the Messiah. Let the building begin!

Chapter One:

God

The purpose of this book is to try to understand how God relates to Israel and the Church and how those two bodies are separate yet interconnected. In order to grasp this important subject, let us begin by addressing the topic of God. The Church knows a lot about biblical topics such as giving, sowing seeds, and the Holy Spirit, but there is one important thing (which the Jews already know) that the Church has not really discovered yet. Both Jews and Arabs tend to be very confused when they hear Christians talking about this one topic that is the key to everything— God.

One biblical prophecy, which is especially scary to me as a Jew, is found in Zechariah 8:23: *"This is what the Lord Almighty says: 'In those days ten men from all languages and nations will take firm hold of one Jew by the hem of his robe* [his *tzitztit*] *and say, "Let us go with you because we have heard that God is with you."'"* Although Zechariah prophesied in the Fifth Century BCE about something that has not yet happened, there is no doubt that his words will come to pass. Every word that God's mouth spoke to the Prophets will not fall to the ground void. One of the reasons that this prophecy must be fulfilled is that the world needs to learn again who God is. In modern Christianity, we have so forgotten the importance of the Father that we are in danger of idolatry. It is as if we have "sent the Father to Acapulco for vacation." We almost never talk about the Father, although we sing about the Holy Spirit saving us and Yeshua as our Lord. We have not gotten to know the Father, yet who God is and who we are worshipping is the key to everything.

So what do we really know about the one true God? The first thing that we need to remember when we are awake and asleep, when we walk on the highway, and when we talk to our children is that, *"In the beginning, God created the heavens and the earth"* (Gen. 1:1). That is how the Bible starts, and it is a simple thing we teach to our children. This truth is the key for understanding Yeshua and the Holy Spirit and the work of salvation. Anyone who forgets the Creator is lost and will go back to idolatry. Anyone who does not really know God is an idol-worshipping pagan, even if he or she sings songs to Yeshua and the Holy Spirit and claims salvation. Even someone who was born a Jew is an idol-worshipper if he does not know God.

It says in Hebrews 11:6, *"Without faith it is impossible to please God, because anyone who comes to him must believe that he exists and that he rewards those who earnestly seek him."* One cannot do right without being rewarded, and one cannot do wrong without being punished. That is the nature of God, and since He is our creator, He owns us.

God created not only the earth, but also the heavens. In 1961, the Russian cosmonaut Yuri Gagarin was the first man to go into space. The space ship *Sputnik* in which he traveled was so small that it was only the size of a pulpit. While he was crouched inside, he looked out of a peephole in the capsule and said, "I am out in the heavens and do not see God." He could not see God in his youth, strength, and cynicism. Several years later, however, his perspective changed because he suffered for years in a hospital from a terrible disease. Right before he died in 1968, he said to the Russian Orthodox priest who was with him, "Now I see God." He did not see God's glory in his creation, but he saw God's mercy in his time of suffering.

Rashi, one of the great Jewish commentators who lived in France and Germany in the Eleventh Century, once asked the question, "Why did God start the Bible with the story of creation?" He could have started directly with the story of Abraham after all. Between chapters 1 and 12 of Genesis, humanity fell three times: the Garden of Eden, the Flood, and the Tower of Babel. What is the purpose of all these stories? There are no commandments in these chapters, so all one can do is study the narratives. Rashi says the reason God started the Bible with, "*In the beginning, God created the heavens and the earth,*" is that one day the wicked people of this world will ask God, "By what right do you give this land to the children of Israel?" He will then say, "I created the world. The world is mine, and I can do with it whatever I want. I can give grace to whomever I want to give grace." This explanation of Rashi's, of course, is only one reason why the book of Genesis begins with this foundational verse. Another explanation is that the entire book that follows (the whole Bible) is meant to witness to the existence of God to all of humanity. The people of Israel are one medium through which God reveals Himself and his ways to the world.

God's creation is incredibly amazing and complex. I know a computer scientist who ran the computers of McDonnell Douglas for many years. He once told me about the rare Cray Super-Computer that McDonnell Douglas had. This computer was one of the top computers in existence several years ago, and there are not very many of them in the world. Only the Pentagon, McDonnell Douglas, and a few universities in the world own these giant super-computers. Nevertheless, this man also told me that the tiny head of a household ant has more computing power than a hundred of these sophisticated computers.

God created the world, so everything in the world is his. This even includes the worst pests in the world like mosquitoes and bedbugs because they too were created and designed by God. God created the ants and the elephants that step on the ants, and when the elephants step on the ants, it does not happen without God's knowledge. Everything, which happens to us in our lives, is under God's control, and nothing that happens in the world is outside of his knowledge. He knew the end of all things before they even began. He knows the number of the hairs on our heads or how many hairs we are missing. God knows everything, and He, not the devil, is in control of his creation. In Western Christianity, we have given too much credit to the devil. There is nothing that pleases the devil more than to have the Church over-occupied with him because the more time we spend being occupied with the devil, the less time we have to spend being occupied with the Almighty God, Creator of the heavens and the earth.

Some people say that Judaism, unlike Christianity, does not have any dogmas. Contrarily, the German Jewish philosopher Franz Rosenweig states that Judaism definitely has dogmas, but not as many as Christianity. The belief in reward and punishment and eternal life, for example, could be thought of as Jewish dogmas, even if they are not traditionally presented in formal creeds. In truth, *the* biblical dogma, the breath of life in every Jew, is the declaration of faith that appears in Deuteronomy 6:4, which is the next key principle for us to remember. It is the most crucial idea of all: *"Shema Yisrael Hashem Elokeynu, Hashem Echad!"* [*"Hear oh Israel, the Lord our God is one Lord!"*] (Deut. 6:4)

If a person concludes with more than one God in his heart at the end of all the calculations and discussion about Yeshua, the Father, the Son, the Holy Spirit, and the Trinity, then he is a heretic, even if he is a Jew. The end conclusion must somehow be one God. The New Testament says that there is only one God fifty three times, yet somehow we have accepted traditions invented by men, instead of accepting what the Word of God says. We have accepted the decisions of fallible human beings at Nicea as more authoritative than the Word of God.

The Word of God is not so complicated. Paul says for example in Romans 3:29-30, *"Is God the God of the Jews only? Is he not the God of the Gentiles too? Yes, of the Gentiles too, since there is only one God, who will justify the circumcised by faith and the uncircumcised through that same faith."* Paul knew and preached the truth very clearly here. Any Jew who forgets that God is the creator of all mankind also forgets that there is only one God. God has no illegitimate children. He created all people, and He loves all of them. If there is only one God, then we are all his children, and we are all brothers.

Paul says in the first half of 1 Corinthians 8:6, *"Yet for us there is but one God, the Father from whom all things came and for whom we live…"* The word "but" means "only" in this verse. This is a very powerful statement that asks us to answer the question, "For whom do we live?" In a way, I live for my children, and my son would say that he lives for his dog. It is great to have children and dogs, but we do not live for these things. According to Paul, we live for God, and He is the reason for our existence. He is the one who made us and is thus responsible for taking care of us and feeding us. Some people might be tempted to say, "He is not feeding me; I work to make a living." My question for that person though is, "Are you sure you will wake up to go to work tomorrow morning?" Our lives are dependant on God; we need his supervision and blessing every day. Paul says to the Athenians in Acts 17:28, *"In him we live and move and have our being..."* Without God there is no guarantee that we will have a tomorrow or even a tonight. If we live for anything else, then we are living for less than our intended purpose.

In the second half of 1 Corinthians 8:6, Paul says, *"...And there is but one Lord, Yeshua the Messiah, through whom all things came and through whom we live."* Notice there is a difference. We live *for* God, *through* the power of Yeshua the Messiah. Through Yeshua the Messiah, we have the ability to live for God because, *"No man comes to the Father except through me,"* as Yeshua said in John 14:6.

There is no conflict between the two halves of 1 Corinthians 8:6. There is only one God and one Father, but there is also only one Lord. Through this Lord, Yeshua the Messiah, we live for God. The idea of referring to Yeshua as "Lord" rests on a few prophetic passages that refer to the Messiah as "Lord," such as Malachi 3:1, *"'Behold I send my messenger to prepare the way before me. The Lord whom you seek will suddenly come to his temple, the messenger of the covenant whom you delight in. Behold he shall come,' says the Lord of Hosts."* Another key text for this title is Psalm 110:1, *"The Lord said to my lord, 'Sit at my right hand until I make your enemies a footstool for your feet.'"* The Lord Yeshua is the instrument that makes it possible for us to live for God because if we are impure and sinful and without the Holy Spirit, unsanctified and defiled by the world, we cannot even approach God. God is a consuming fire, and we cannot approach Him with sin. We first have to accept the Messiah as the instrument that cleanses us, brings us to the Father, and makes it possible for us to have an encounter with the Almighty God, the Creator of the universe. We believe in the Father, the Son, and the Holy Spirit because both the Hebrew Bible and the New Testament teach that they were part of the revelation of God to the people of Israel long before Yeshua was born in Bethlehem.

Many of the New Testament passages about the Father and the Son — including the ones in Colossians, Ephesians, and Hebrews that talk about Yeshua as the Creator of the world — are derived from Proverbs 30:4. It asks the following questions: *"Who has gone up into heaven and come down? Who has gathered up the wind in the hollow of his hands? Who has wrapped up the waters in his cloak? Who has established the ends of the earth? What is his name and the name of his son? Tell me if you know."* The first half of this short passage asks a lot of questions about the power behind creation, and the answer to all of the questions in the first half is "God." God created the earth, just as the Bible starts, *"In the beginning, God created the heavens and the earth."* Yet Proverbs says that He has a son. Several other places in the Old Testament, such as Psalm 2, also speak of God having a son.

What does it mean that God and his son participated together in the creation of the world? As a result of polemical disputes with Christianity, Jewish tradition has abandoned this idea of participation in creation and consigned it to the realm of idolatrous beliefs. The idea of participation appears as early as the story of creation, however, in which God says in the plural, not in the singular, *"Let us make man in our image"* (Gen. 1:26). Here God is apparently speaking with some other party during the process of Creation. This verse that uses "the language of man" does not mean there are multiple gods, although this confusion has led to various interpretations of this verse.

There is only one God who is unique, there is no other beside Him, and yet He has a Son with Whom He cooperates. There is absolute equality between the Father and the Son. He who has seen the Son has also seen the Father, according to John 14:9, and there is absolute equality between them because Yeshua said in John 10:30, *"I and the Father are one."* The problem is that if one leaves it just at "equality," then one ends up with two gods. This is complicated yet crucial. If the Father and the Son are only equal to each other, there are two equal beings with equal power, authority, and nature. That makes them two equal gods, one beside the other. If one of them is under the other, however, and one receives his authority, character, nature, and mission from the other, there is only one God expressing himself by his equal. This is the meaning of John 17:3 when it says, *"Now this is eternal life: that they may know you the only true God, and Yeshua the Messiah, whom you have sent."*

Yeshua continually repeats throughout the Gospels that everything He does and says is not of his own accord and authority, but rather on the authority of the Father. One example of this sort of statement appears in John 14:24, 28, which says, *"These words you hear are not my own; they belong to the Father who sent me."* In John 17:24, on the night before Yeshua was crucified, He cried, prayed, and sweated drops of blood in the Garden of Gethsemane: *"Father, I want those you have given me to be with me where I am and to see my glory, the glory you have given me because you loved me before the creation of the world."* This text in John is based on the conversation between Moses and God on the subject of knowing God through the revelation of his face in Exodus

33. If Moses needed the revelation of the face of God in order to reach the knowledge of Him, how much more should we be sure that every ordinary person needs it, too. Besides these texts, Yeshua Himself also said that the Father is greater than the Son in John 14:28: *"The Father is greater than I."* In other words, there is equality and also hierarchy. Modern Western thinkers have a hard time understanding this because we have been trained to think like Greeks and not like Jews. Greek logic says that if A=B and B=C, then it has to be that A=C. It is not necessarily so, however, in theology. God is far too complex to limit Him to the rules of a geometry proof.

For example, men and women are equal to each other according to Galatians 3:28, *"There is neither Jew nor Greek, slave nor free, male nor female."* We are equal to each other before God, yet at the same time Ephesians 5:22 says, *"Wives, submit to your husbands as to the Lord."* There is equality and hierarchy at the same time, and one does not necessarily violate the other. *"The husband shall cleave to his wife, and they shall be one flesh,"* (Genesis 2:24), but in spite of being one flesh and being equal, they have a relationship of subordination based on love, rather than on dictatorship. There is a big difference between being subordinate in a loving relationship and being subordinate in a dictatorship, so it is possible to have a relationship of equality and subordination at the same time.

Many believers also misinterpret this verse in Galatians 3:28 to mean that God no longer desires for Jews to express their distinctive identity, thereby turning the Church into one homogeneous body in which one cannot tell the difference between Jews and Greeks. Just as men and women retain their distinctive genders after marriage, a Jew who believes in Yeshua does not stop being a Jew or become exactly the same as a Greek. The point of the verse is that both Jews and Greeks, men and women, and slaves and free people have exactly the same standing and value before God. The Midrash Eliyahu Rabbah says something interestingly similar to this in its discussion on Deborah the judge and prophetess of Israel. *"'Now Deborah, a prophetess... judged Israel at that time.'* (Judg. 4:4) In reference to this verse, it should be noted that Phineas, the son of Eleazar, was still serving Israel in Deborah's time as judge and prophet. Hence it may be asked: What was the special character of Deborah that she, too, judged Israel and prophesied concerning them? In regard to her deeds, I call heaven and earth to witness that whether it be a heathen or a Jew, whether it be a man or a woman, a manservant or a maidservant, the holy spirit will suffuse each of them in keeping with the deeds he or she performs."[1]

Another point that needs to be made clear is that this identification of the unity of the Father and the Son, between the messenger and the one who sends the message, is not an invention of the New Testament writers. This unity also exists in the Hebrew Scriptures. Unfortunately, all too often Christians and Messianic Jews are so eager to prove the concept of the Trinity from the Hebrew Bible that they rip verses out of context and use all the wrong passages for their apologetic purposes. This misuse of verses, which were never intended to be read that way, only further distances the hearers from the Gospel and causes them to lose respect for the way believers interpret and read the Bible. Thus, before using an Old Testament verse for apologetics one should check and double check the context and the message to make sure one is using it correctly. For example, one cannot say that Isaiah

---

1   Eliyahu Rabbah p. 48 or chapter (9) 10. This translation comes from *Tanna Debe Eliyyahu.* Translated by William C. Braude and Israel J. Kapstein. Philadelphia: JPS, 1981, pp. 112-113.

6:3 "proves the Trinity" because it says, *"Holy, holy, holy is the Lord of Hosts; the whole earth is full of his glory."* Using an adjective such as "holy" three times is a well-known literary phenomenon that increases the level of holiness in the description. It is similar to a superlative, like "holiest" and has no bearing on whether God is one, three, five, or ten. There are many other examples of foolish interpretations of the Hebrew Bible that the Church and even Messianic Jews use far too often, but we will limit ourselves here to this fairly obvious negative example so the point can be easily understood. This sort of ill-founded interpretation only makes believers look foolish and naive. It is better to do one's homework before embarking on an apologetic mission because the last thing we want to do is to distance people from the truth through our flawed interpretations.

None of these statements are meant to contradict or to take away from Yeshua's divine nature, but rather to understand it more perfectly. There are a number of texts from the Hebrew Scriptures that do affirm the close identification among God and the Messiah and Israel, between the sender and the messenger, and that blur the boundaries nearly completely. For example, one verse that has clear implications for the Divine nature of the Messiah is Zechariah 2:10-12, which says, *"'Sing and rejoice, O daughter of Zion, for behold I come and I will dwell in your midst,' declares the Lord. 'And many nations shall join themselves to the Lord in that day and shall be my people. And I will dwell in your midst, and you shall know that the Lord of Hosts has sent me to you.'"* This verse speaks about God sending the Messiah, Whom He clearly identifies with Himself. If one simply tries to look at the grammar of the pronouns in this passage, it looks like a mess, but when we understand that the "I" who will dwell among Israel is the Messiah, it becomes clear that the Messiah is identified with God.

Another very interesting passage on the subject of the Divine nature of the Messiah and how the nations will come to worship the true God through the Messiah appears in Isaiah 45:14-25. Although it is long, it is worth quoting at length. *"Thus says the Lord: 'The wealth of Egypt and the merchandise of Cush, and the Sabeans, men of stature, shall come over to you and be yours; they shall follow you. They shall come over in chains and bow down to you. They will plead with you saying, "Surely God is in you, and there is no other, no god besides him." ' Truly, you are a God who hides yourself, O God of Israel, the Savior. All of them are put to shame and confounded; the makers of idols go in confusion together. But Israel is saved by the Lord with everlasting salvation; you shall not be put to shame or confounded to all eternity. For thus says the Lord, who created the heavens, (he is God!), who formed the earth and established it. He did not create it empty; he formed it to be inhabited. 'I am the Lord, and there is no other. I did not speak in secret, in a land of darkness. I did not say to the offspring of Jacob, "Seek me in vain." I the Lord speak truth; I declare what is right. Assemble yourselves and come; draw near together, you survivors of the nations! They have no knowledge who carry about their wooden idols and keep on praying to a god that cannot save. Declare and present your case; let them take counsel together. Who told this long ago? Who declared it of old? Was it not I the Lord? And there is no other god besides me, a righteous God and a Savior; there is none beside me. Turn to me and be saved, all the ends of the earth! For I am God, and there is no other. By myself I have sworn; from my mouth has gone out in righteousness, a word that shall not return: "To me every knee shall bow and every tongue shall swear allegiance." Only in the Lord, it shall be said of me, are righteousness and strength; to him shall come and be ashamed all who were incensed against him. In the Lord all the offspring of Israel shall be justified and shall glory.'"*

This passage talks a great deal about God's salvation and how the only salvation will come through Him. Yeshua, whose very name means *salvation*, is the only Savior both for Jews and non-Jews, yet God makes it clear in this passage that He is the only God that there is. It is through their knowledge of Yeshua, the Messiah of Israel, that the nations who used to be enslaved to idolatry are gradually coming to know and worship the true God. Although many Christians wish to disconnect themselves and God from Israel, they will eventually see the presence of God in Israel. The pagan nations will also, at some point, have to submit to the one true God and the Messiah of Israel to whom *"every knee shall bow and every tongue shall swear allegiance."* Clearly this passage is the background behind Philippians 2:5-11, which says, *"Have this mind among yourselves, which is yours in the Messiah Yeshua, who, though he was in the form of God, did not count equality with God a thing to be grasped but made himself nothing, taking the form of a servant, being born in the likeness of men. And being found in human form, he humbled himself by becoming obedient to the point of death, even death on a cross. Therefore God has highly exalted him and bestowed on him the name that is above every name, so that at the name of Yeshua every knee should bow, in heaven and on earth and under the earth, and every tongue confess that Yeshua the Messiah is Lord, to the glory of God the Father."*

These passages alone obligate us to seriously consider the idea of the divinity of the Messiah and his unity with God.

Many New Testament "experts" today and a growing number of Jewish people mistakenly think that because the Judaism of the Second Temple Period was not expecting a divine Messiah that the first generation of the Church did not believe in the divinity of Yeshua either because of their fear of idolatry. This theory holds that Paul invented the idea of Yeshua being the Son of God because he did not care about the unity of God and so introduced idolatry into the Church. We have seen that the divine nature of the Messiah can be found even in the Hebrew Scriptures, however, so there was no need for Paul to invent it. Paul insisted on the divine nature of the Messiah in his writings, but he also saw absolutely no contradiction between the unity of God and the divinity of the Messiah. In Galatians 3:20 he says, *"Now an intermediary implies more than one, but God is one."* One of the most important parts of Paul's mission to the Gentiles was to bring monotheism to the pagan world that was lost in the slavery and darkness of idolatry, as Isaiah 9:2 says, *"The people who walked in darkness have seen a great light; those who dwelt in a land of deep darkness, on them light has shined."*

These things do not need to contradict each other when read in their correct context, just as Paul knew well. The common identity between the sender and the messenger, the Father and the Son, appears several times in the Prophets, but both Yeshua and the Prophets also express the idea of a common identity between the Messiah and Israel. We therefore stand in front of a great triangle of common identities among the Father, the Son, and Israel, which we cannot ever separate from each other.

Believers today need to return to their roots and the truth of the Bible before Yeshua returns. It takes courage to learn new things, and we are all in the process of learning, discovering, and restoring our faith to its pure source. All too often people do not know what is under their feet, and they have accepted false traditions as truths because no one has told them otherwise.

One of the terrible curses in the Bible is to trust in men while having the illusion of trusting in God, as it says in Jeremiah 17:5-9: *"This is what the LORD says, 'Cursed is the one who trusts in man, who depends on flesh for his strength and whose heart turns away from the LORD. He will be like a bush in the wastelands; he will not see prosperity when it comes. He will dwell in the parched places of the desert, in a salt land, where no one lives. But blessed is the man who trusts in the LORD, whose confidence is in him. He will be like a tree planted by the water that sends out its roots by the stream. It does not fear when heat comes; its leaves are always green. It has no worries in a year of drought and never fails to bear fruit. The heart is deceitful above all things and beyond cure. Who can understand it?' "*

This text is like the fine print in a life insurance policy because human beings are generally lazy. We want everything instantly, and there are plenty of charlatans in the world who promise instant salvation without the recipient having to do anything. This is not the same thing as being saved through the grace of God as a free gift. We may be saved through grace, but that does not mean we are supposed to slide through the rest of our lives without making any efforts toward righteousness, holiness, and good works. Our efforts are important because it is our good works that prepare and fit us for the presence of God and that build the kingdom of heaven. Most of today's popular preachers do not preach a life of good works and only want to emphasize the "free gift" of salvation that we should receive, since no one wants to hear that they need to work hard to please God.

On the contrary, I get scared when someone says to me, "I am going to give you something, and you do not have to do anything for it." I learned better than that when my son was born. Since my wife is diabetic, she had a lot of trouble during pregnancy. We were very poor but, in spite of that, decided to go to the best doctor in Israel. When he accepted us, we were very happy that he was going to take care of my wife during her pregnancy and do the Caesarean, but I kept asking, "Doctor, how much is this going to cost me?"

He kept answering, "I'm a doctor, and I don't talk about money. Don't worry about it." I believed him, but after the surgery he told me how much it was going to cost. Then I said to him, "Ok, now you can start worrying because I don't have that kind of money." Nothing good in life is free; even if it comes free to us, it has cost someone something.

There are too many pastors who promise instant salvation and tell people not to do any *mitzvot* [commandments] or good deeds and say, "Salvation is by grace, and God does not expect you to do anything. Keeping his commandments is of no value." Trusting those pastors who seek the glory of God for themselves and fleece the flocks and teach the people falsely will only bring a curse. Anyone who trusts in other people will be cursed. This sounds cynical, but one cannot argue with Jeremiah, the inspired prophet of God. We can either trust or not trust the Word of God. The Bible never says, "Put your trust in men, and trust the used car salesman." Instead, it says, *"Cursed is the man who puts his trust in men. He will be like a tree planted in the desert, in salty land. His leaves will wither, and he will bear no fruit."*

Swallowing Christian creeds whole without critically comparing them to the truth of the Bible will only bring the curse of being like that withered tree in Jeremiah. We have the whole Bible, so we need to learn to use it. Nearly everyone in the Western world now has the opportunity to learn how to read the Bible. The ability of the masses to read is a tremendous blessing that was unknown in previous generations of history, so we should take advantage of this great gift of literacy to read the Bible for ourselves and see what God expects from us.

Although the Bible emphasizes that God is One, we also believe that Yeshua is divine. As a Jew, I can still believe that Yeshua is the Deity because of passages like Jeremiah 23:5-6 that says the name of the Messiah will be *"the LORD, our righteousness."* Both Rabbi David Kimchi (Radak) and the Targum Jonathan on this passage explain that this verse refers to the King Messiah. Isaiah 9:5-6 says the name of the Messiah will be *"Wonderful Counselor, Mighty God, Father of Eternity, Prince of Peace."* The Talmud in tractate Baba Batra 75b also quotes Jeremiah 23:6 when it says that the Messiah will be named after God Himself and will be called "the LORD our righteousness." If Jews can say that the name of the Messiah is "the LORD our righteousness," then there is no problem with believing that Yeshua is God. He is God in such a way, however, that He does not compromise the oneness of God.

The unity of God is important not just for the sake of doctrinal purity; rather it has great ethical and spiritual implications that we must grasp. The ethical connection to the unity of God is visible in the words of the prophet Malachi. One passage in Malachi that does not deal with offerings touches on the subject of the Fatherhood of God. When most Christians hear a reference to Malachi, they automatically start reaching for their wallets to put their tithes in the offering plate, yet that is not the only point of the book. In Malachi 2:10, the prophet says to the people of Judah, *"Have we not all one Father? Did not one God create us? Why do we profane the covenant of our fathers by breaking faith with one another?"* That is an important question because believing in one God is not only a question of theology. There was no systematic Jewish theology until the 20th Century. The liberal German Jews who studied in Christian seminaries are the ones who wrote the first Jewish theologies in the 20th Century. This statement is not just important because it fits nicely into a systematic theology. Malachi wrote this because being a monotheist has practical implications for daily life for families, businesses, and congregations. If there is one God who is the Father of us all, then we must not *"break faith with one another."*

Knowing that there is only one God and only one ultimate authority for everything that happens in the world makes a person responsible for his deeds because there is no escaping to the territory of another deity. It is not like children who go to their mother to ask for something after their father has already said "no." There is only one Authority, the Father of us all, and there is no getting away from Him. So what does Malachi mean here about "breaking faith with one another"? He means causing distrust, not being loyal or committed to one another, and not taking care of one another. That is what he calls "breaking the covenant."

If we believed in one God, there would be no racism because God created us all. If we believed in one God, there would be no abuse because we would realize that everybody is God's child and that we are brothers. If we believed in one God, married people would love each other unconditionally and would not run after sexual temptations whenever things become difficult in their marriages. If we believed in one God, there would be no poverty, except for the lazy who do not want to work.

Believing in one God who created everyone makes us brothers and sisters with no room for prejudice. Prejudice, in fact, denies the oneness of God because it claims that some human beings are not our brothers. If they are not our brothers, then we are somebody else's children, and we all have different fathers. If God is the Father of us all, however, we are brothers whether we like it or not.

Believing in one God and that Yeshua, our Lord whom God sent to the world, existed before creation is very important. The Jews believe that the Messiah existed before the creation of the world, and the New Testament teaches this too because it is a Jewish book. God already knew the disease and produced the cure for the disease of humanity before He even created mankind.

Non-Jewish Christians need to remember that before Christianity reached Europe, their forefathers worshipped idols and were far from the knowledge of the true God. They stopped worshipping idols when they believed in Yeshua the Messiah and, through Him, came to the knowledge of the Father. Ephesians 2:13 says, *"But now in Yeshua the Messiah you who once were far away have been brought near through the blood of the Messiah."* Both their sins and the sins of the Jews were forgiven through the blood of Yeshua. Through Yeshua the Messiah, they were introduced to the Bible and became one with God's people, not replacing Israel, but rather joining with Israel. They joined them by faith and became the seed of Abraham. The kingdom of God only has places for children of Abraham. A non-Jew who is not a child of Abraham by faith has not entered into the covenant. According to the covenant God made with Abraham, Gentiles come into the covenant based on faith and not by circumcision or keeping the Law. According to Ephesians 2:13, those who have faith in Yeshua have joined the covenant with Israel but have not replaced Israel. The second crucial element in this triangle of "God, Israel, and the Church" is Israel and how it works together with the Church for God's glory in history. Due to the Church's tragically long misunderstanding of this relationship, we will examine this further in the next chapter.

What happened in Christian history was that the Church said they had become "Spiritual Israel." The word "spiritual" stands for "virtual." According to this understanding, non-Jewish believers are "cyber-Jews" or "virtual Jews." That theory may sound good, but it is not in the Word of God. The Christian faith is inseparably tied to the Jewish people. We believe in a Jew who died for us on the cross. Nobody took his life; He gave it because He knew what his duty was. He knew what the will of the Father was, and He was willing to be obedient to the Father, just as we should be obedient to Him.

One more verse about this specific point is Hebrews 5:8: *"Although he was a son, he learned obedience from what he suffered."* Yeshua had to learn obedience; He could have disobeyed and fallen to the temptations of the devil. When the devil met Him in the wilderness after forty days of hunger and thirst and said, "Make these stones into bread," Yeshua could have said, "Yes, I'll make them into French toast." When Satan said, "I'll give you the kingdoms of the earth," Yeshua could have taken his offer. The temptation was not a theater; it was for real. The important thing is that He did not yield to the temptation. The man was hungry, thirsty, and tired after forty days in a very harsh wilderness. Nevertheless, *"He learned obedience from what he suffered and, once made perfect, he became the source of eternal salvation for all those who obey him."[1]*

No one is saved by works. One prayer in the Jewish prayer book that is recited on every fast day says, *"Avinu Malkeynu, chaneynu v'aneynu, ki eyn banu ma'asim. Asei imanu tzedaka v'chesed v'hoshieynu."* This means, "Our Father, our King, have mercy upon us and answer us because we do not have any good deeds. Deal with us in righteousness and mercy and save us." Christians are good at knowing that deeds cannot save them, but if a person does not do anything after he "gets saved," then he is not really saved at all. We must be obedient to God's commands because Yeshua said, *"If you love me, you will keep my commands"* (John 14:15). We are not saved by the commandments, but we have to show our love by doing and giving. There is no love if there is no giving.

Because there is one God in whom we trust, we also should give a little bit of grace and benefit of the doubt to our fellow man, even knowing that if he does not cheat us, it is a miracle. We believe in miracles because we believe that God can take evil people and turn their hearts around, save them, and make them obedient servants. Yeshua learned obedience by the things from which He suffered, and then He became the author of eternal salvation for all those who obey Him. There is no faith in God without obedience. Paul himself repeats many times, "According to the Law, I am blameless," in Philippians 3 among other places. What does it mean to say "I am blameless"? To be blameless according to the Law means to keep the Torah, yet it is not enough to keep the Torah. A person cannot be saved by keeping the Torah because that is the minimum. Yeshua said, *"Unless your righteousness exceeds that of the Pharisees and the teachers of the Law you*

1   Hebrews 5:8-9

will not enter the kingdom of Heaven" (Matt. 5:20). We have to be better, more obedient, more faithful, and more loyal than they were. That is the only way the Church is going to provoke the Jews to jealousy. Only when they see that we love God and the Torah and each other more than they do will they see who Yeshua really is.

First of all, we have to know who God is, where we come from, and about our responsibility to our brothers and sisters. Next we will look at why God elected Israel. Personally, if I were God, I would not have chosen Israel; I would have chosen the Japanese because they are far more efficient. Because God chose Israel, we have been trying to run away from our responsibility for thousands of years. Nevertheless, Israel is and always will be God's chosen people to bring the message of monotheism to the world.

The Church is expected to bring the world to God through Yeshua. We live in a world of idolatry and racial hatred, so we must help spread the glory of the one God throughout the world in order to solve these problems. No matter how much one calculates and theologizes, the end conclusion must be *Shema Yisrael… "Hear oh Israel, the LORD our God is one LORD!"*

Chapter Two:

Israel

The second side of the triangle of relationships which we are discussing in this book is the people of Israel—that is, the Jews. God chose the Jews to be his special people thousands of years ago when He called Abraham. The nations of the world have resented his choice ever since then and fought against his will by rebelling against Him and persecuting his people. His choice does not mean that the Jews were better than the other peoples of the world, back then or today, but it means that they have a special task and calling as mediators between God and the nations. God also chose the Church, but somehow many Christians do not understand their place in his plan and therefore resent or deny the choice of Israel. This resentment led to many horrible acts of Christian anti-Semitism throughout history and ultimately stems from an identity crisis.

People who do not know who they are suffer a lot. Teenagers who find out that they were adopted and do not know their biological parents, even if they were surrounded by love and have been well taken care of, are suddenly willing to do everything to find out who they really are. People today are obsessed with defining their identity, "finding themselves," and their "place in this world" because they have completely lost the sense of their true identity as the servants and creations of God.

Part of the problem of Western Christianity is exactly that. I have nearly fifteen church histories on my bookshelf. So many of the Protestant Evangelical Church history books start with the Reformation—with Luther, with Zwingli, with Huss, and with Calvin. None of these men started Christianity though, and thousands of years of God's interactions with mankind passed into history before the Protestant Reformers came into the world. A Church that begins only with the Reformation has no roots and no real identity. What has happened today is that a lot of Christians are walking around dazed without roots or identities because they know nothing about the Church before the Reformation. They do not know where they came from or why they are even Christians.

Being Christian is the thing to do in a so-called Christian country like the United States. Society says that going to church is good for the children, so people go to church. Many people decide, "We'll find a church that we like, with a bunch of people that we get along with, and we'll take our family to church because that is the American thing to do." That is what is expected of a good upright citizen. Then all of a sudden they wake up one morning and ask, "Who am I? Where did I come from? Why do I believe in Yeshua? Why do I believe in God?"

In 1975, I was in New York and taught a number of specialized seminars for about six weeks. Each week was for a different group of people. One week was for unbelievers, one week for evangelists, one week for the theologians from the different seminaries in New York, and one week was for the Messianic Jewish leadership. During that time in New York, I found out that even though most of the people who came to the seminars were raised in so-called Christian homes, they did not really know who they were, why they believed in God, or how to really answer their fellow man for the hope that God had put in them.

Part of the reason for this confusion is that the worldwide Church denied its origins and its roots sometime in the Fourth Century. They got embarrassed by who the parents of their faith really were and so cut themselves off from their roots. Christians in those days became embarrassed by the fact that they believed in the God of Abraham, Isaac, and Jacob. They became embarrassed that Yeshua was a Jew because it was not very popular to be a Jew at that time. Jews were a nation spread out in the Diaspora. Their country was occupied by Romans, and the city of Jerusalem was deleted from the map. The Roman Emperor Hadrian destroyed it in 135 CE, rebuilt it as a totally pagan city into which Jews were not allowed to enter, and changed its name to Aeolia Capitolina. "Capitolina" came from the Capitol Hill in Rome, and "Aeolias" was Hadrian's family name. Jews had no home, no administration, and no government, so the Church preferred to find grace in the eyes of the Roman Empire.

They started saying, "Wait a minute, where is Jerusalem? Why should we look toward Jerusalem? Rome is our capitol. Rome is the center of our faith. We owe nothing to the Jews because of what they did. They killed our God!" Thus, they denied their roots and drifted further and further away from Israel.

They could not drift very far while reading the Bible, of course, because every time they opened the Bible, they saw things like, *"For God will save Zion and will build the cities of Judah, and he will dwell there and inherit it"* (Psalm 69:36). In other places it talks about Elisha speaking to the King of Israel, or in the New Testament in Romans 10:1 it says *"Brothers, my heart's desire and prayer to God for Israel is that they may be saved."* Even the New Testament talks about Bethlehem, Hebron, Jerusalem, Nazareth, Caesarea, and Jaffa. Nowhere in the Bible is there anything about Paris because Paris did not exist then. There is nothing in the Bible about the Twin Towers in New York or about Portland, Oregon either.

Since the Church could not officially stop reading the Bible, they had to work hard to separate themselves from Israel and try to replace it. They continued to read the Bible but instead of interpreting it literally, they began to spiritualize it. They turned everything concrete and real into allegories, and even things as obviously physical as the Jordan River became allegorical. Think of a song that is sung about the Jordan River in church, such as "You won't have to cross Jordan alone" or "On Jordan's Stormy Banks I Stand." These songs are ridiculous because the Jordan River is only about as wide as four rows of chairs in a church. Some people in America have creeks in their backyard that are wider than the Jordan River, so there is no need to sing hymns about the dangers of crossing it.

So why do Christians sing about the stormy Jordan and "casting a wishful eye on Canaan's Land"? The Jordan River is really used as an adaptation of pagan, Greek myths. In Greek mythology, a dead person had to cross the River Styx to get to the Underworld, and his relatives had to give him a coin in order to cross the river. The Greeks put a coin in the dead person's mouth, so that he could pay the boat-man to ferry him across the river. So when Christians sing, "On Jordan's stormy banks I stand and cast a wishful eye, to Canaan's fair and happy land, where my possessions lie" what do they really mean? They sing about dying and crossing the Jordan River because the Jordan has become a symbol of dying and going to heaven. Crossing from the Eastern to the Western side of the Jordan makes a big difference because one enters the land of Milk and Honey, but it is definitely not heaven. There is still a lot of desert and wilderness there, so it is not the allegorical Paradise people have in mind when they sing these hymns.

By allegorizing and spiritualizing everything, many Christians have taken the Bible out of its reality and put it into cyberspace or Disneyworld. The Bible became a book of allegories because it was taken out of its historical setting and its First Century environment. By spiritualizing and allegorizing the Bible, one can make it say anything he wants, but that robs today's believers of their roots. We are physical beings with real needs, with real pains, with real aspirations, and with real desires to serve in partnership with God in the great work of salvation that Yeshua did. All too often, however, the Church spiritualizes reality and expects people to ignore their real lives and be satisfied with some kind of aspirant placebo. The Bible does not teach that all the blessings and help that God promised to give us will be reserved for post-mortem bliss. Yeshua also promised to give us abundant life in the here and now, which means a lot more than the "Health and Wealth Gospel" that is so popular in certain Christian communities.

Unfortunately, the early Church fathers also decided to take all the curse sections of the Bible and apply them to the Jews and to apply all the blessing sections to themselves. For many years the standard position of the Protestant, Catholic, and Greek Orthodox churches followed this line of thought: "The Jews rejected Yeshua, so God rejected them. He gave their inheritance to the Church, which became Spiritual Israel." If one were to ask most Christians if they are "a part of Spiritual Israel," ninety percent of them would answer affirmatively because that is what they have been taught. Yet the truth is that there is no place in the entire Bible that mentions "Spiritual Israel." There never was such a thing, and there never will be such a thing. This concept was invented by people who allegorized the real Israel and applied it to the Church to make it "Spiritual Israel" or "Virtual Israel."

Contrary to nearly 2,000 years of Christian history, however, the apostle Paul says in Romans 11 that God has not rejected the Jews. Paul says in plain language in Romans 11:1, *"I ask then, did God reject his people? By no means!..."* If we believe in the inspired word of God, that Paul was full of the Holy Spirit, and that God gave him those words, then we have to believe what he says about Israel. He says, *"...By no means! I am an Israelite myself..."* By the way, please note that "I am" is in the present tense in this verse, which proves his belief in Yeshua did not remove him from Israel.

When I first accepted Yeshua as my Lord, on September 2, 1962, the missionaries taught me, "Listen, you were a Jew. Now that you believe in Yeshua you are no longer a Jew. You're no longer obligated to do anything Jewish. If you eat a kosher pickle, you're backsliding." When I told them years later that I no longer ate pork and that I was starting to keep kosher, they said, "You are backsliding."

I innocently asked, "Eating pork will make me more spiritual?"

They said, "We think so."

So I replied, "Then bring out the whole pig, from the tip of his nose all the way to his rear end for me to eat!"

They said, "Ok, ok, we get your point."

This kind of misunderstanding may look ridiculous in this anecdote, but this is exactly the way that most Christians think when it comes to Jews and salvation. On the contrary, Paul said, "I am," not "I was," a Jew. A lot of Jews who believe in Yeshua say, "I was Jewish," but I want to know what they have become now. Perhaps a cocker spaniel or chopped liver—what has happened to them? I cannot stop being Jewish by believing that another Jew is the Son of God. I cannot stop being Jewish by believing that another Jew died for me on the cross, was raised on the third day, and ascended to sit at the right hand of the Father. Paul believed all those things, yet he said, *"I am* [in the present tense] *an Israelite, a descendent of Abraham, from the tribe of Benjamin."* He was born a Jew and proudly remained a Jew for the rest of his life, even if not all of the Jewish community was proud to claim him.

Romans 11:2-5 continues, *"God did not reject his people, whom he foreknew. Don't you know what the Scripture says in the passage about Elijah—how he appealed to God against Israel? 'Lord they have killed your prophets and torn down your altars. I am the only one left, and they are trying to kill me.' And what was God's answer to him? 'I have reserved for myself 7,000 who have not bowed the knee to Baal.' So, too, at the present time there is a remnant chosen by grace."*

Paul quotes this conversation between Elijah and God to prove his point that *"God has not rejected his people [the people of Israel], whom he foreknew."* The context there is the Jewish people, not the believers, but the unbelieving Jews. God has not rejected them, even though they have not received Yeshua. Even though they have not walked faithfully before God, He has not rejected them and has always reserved for Himself a faithful remnant, which preserved the light that God has given Israel, like in the days of Elijah. The remnant Paul referred to here was probably composed of Jewish believers, including himself, but he also made it clear that this remnant did not exist by its own merit or good graces. Rather, *there is a remnant chosen by grace,*[1] and this remnant has no reason to behave proudly toward unbelieving Israel or the rest of the Church.

---

1   Romans 11:3

One of the most destructive doctrines in Christian theology is called Replacement Theology, which says that God has rejected Israel and replaced it with his Church. I would like to ask these Christians, "With which church was it that God replaced Israel—the Catholic Church, the Greek Orthodox Church, the Pentecostal Church, the Baptist Church, or the Non-Denominational Church? Every church or denomination thinks they are the true Church, but God only sees one Church, that is the Body of Messiah as it is composed of many different people and groups. This Church has not replaced Israel, however, no matter how special the Church is to God.

When Paul says, *"God has not rejected his people whom he foreknew,"* he was talking about Israel. From the very beginning, the people of Israel were the chosen people of God. They have always been the chosen people of God, and nobody else was ever chosen in their place. They are still the chosen people of God, but even a chosen person can go to hell. This is a key point. No one was ever chosen to be saved by what we call in Hebrew *proteksia*, (which means getting around the rules by knowing the right person in the right bureaucratic position). No person was ever saved because of who his father or mother is or by what tribe or nation he is from. Election has nothing to do with salvation. Our only *proteksia* comes from the grace of God in giving us a relationship with his Son.

All of Israel was elected, and they all came out of Egypt with Moses. They all crossed through the Red Sea on dry land, ate manna every day, were led by Moses and Aaron, stood under Mt. Sinai, and received the greatest revelation that a group of people has ever received. They all heard the voice of God, literally and physically, not just in a dream. Nevertheless, God swore not to let them into his promised land and into his rest. Psalm 95, which is quoted in Hebrews 3:4 says, *"I swear that they will not enter into my rest."* That is why they all died in the wilderness, except Joshua and Caleb. God's election has to do with functionality, what a person's job is, and not with what his reward is. Salvation is dependant instead on a person's faithfulness to God.

One everyday example is the fact that it is not absolutely necessary for children to inherit their parents' property. Everyone has the right to disinherit his children, and there are parents who have done so, in fact. Nevertheless, they are still their children, and that fact cannot be changed no matter how many times either one of the parties denies it. Even though they may have disinherited their children, they cannot deny the fact that they came out of their loins and out of their wombs and that they are still their children. Similarly, Israel was chosen by God. There are dozens of places in the Bible about Israel being chosen by God, being the apple of God's eye, and being God's prized possession. The Hebrew word translated in English as "prized possession" is a dowry. Israel is God's bride, chosen by God, but it does not mean that every single Jew is automatically saved. Election only means that every Jew has a purpose in history, a job to do, and a calling to fulfill.

Many Christians resist this doctrine of God's election, thinking that if God elected someone, it means He saved him. The truth is that God elected them, and He expects faith, faithfulness, and obedience. If they are not faithful and obedient, they are not saved, although they are still the children of God. Even though everybody is a part of the children of God and every nation under the earth is a part of God's people, his election was only for Israel.

A very interesting passage in Amos 3:2, which many Jews do not like to read because of its implications, talks about Israel in this way: *"You only have I chosen of all the families of the earth. Therefore I will punish you for all your sins."* Every Jew is happy to hear the first half, *"You only have I chosen from all the nations of the earth,"* yet nobody is happy to hear the second half, *"Therefore I will punish you for all your sins."* Unfortunately, the second half of the verse is just as true as the first. No nation has gone through the suffering that the Jews have in the last 2,000 years of history, and no nation has paid the price of unbelief as much as the Jews have.

Many people in the Western world have the impression that the world is all Christian. On the contrary, Christianity is not the largest religion in the world, and it never has been! Today the fastest growing religion, even larger than Christianity, is Islam. Fifteen years ago there were more Christians in the world than Muslims, but now there are more Muslims than Christians. Even if one combines the Jews, the Muslims, and the Christians together, monotheists still compose barely a third of the world's population. More than half of the world or even two-thirds of the world are still idol-worshipping pagans: Buddhists, Shintoists, and Hindus who do not believe in Yeshua, Mohammed, or Moses. Tragically, Christianity is still a minority in the world, and yet it keeps dividing and subdividing again within itself instead of addressing the crisis of idolatry and darkness. Everybody talks about unity but continues to divide. Everybody says, "Let's unite," but nobody is willing to give up any of their traditions and practices or learn anything new from the Word of God. They all come to the table of unity with their preconceived ideas and preconditions and refuse to take hold of their greater mission.

I am nothing and my people are nothing. We are clay in the hands of the Almighty God, and He has dealt with us according to his will. He told our prophets thousands of years ago, "If you disobey me, I will kick you out of the Land," and He did it. We did not want to leave the Land He gave to Abraham, but He brought the enemy to remove us. Similarly, when it was his timing, He brought us back to the Land, whether we wanted to come or not.

My father, who is no longer living, was a total unbeliever and an atheist. He did not like God, he did not like religion, and, worst of all, he did not like religious Jews. He could tolerate the Christians, but he could not even tolerate religious Jews. Still he left a good job, a nice home in downtown Sofia, Bulgaria, packed up his baggage and his babies (I was less than two years old), and went to the Land of Israel that he had never even visited before. He did not like the neighborhood, the neighbors, or being in the Middle East. He was a European, and he wanted to remain a European. What made him and thousands of other Jews like him do it? God brought the Jews back to the Land, and many of them asked, "What am I doing here? Why am I here?" Only after they believed in God did they realize what God was doing among them in resurrecting the State of Israel and the people of Israel.

The same thing is true with the Church. Most people in the Church do not know where they belong, and they are asking themselves, "Where does God want me? What does God want from me?" We are all in the hands of God and have a duty to carry out his purposes for our lives.

Let us now look at some of the purposes for which God elected the Jews. There are a number of times in the Prophets where God says very clearly why He chose us. Isaiah 42:6-8 states, *"I, the Lord, have called you* [the Jewish people] *in righteousness. I will take hold of your hand. I will keep you and will make you to be a covenant for the people and a light for the Gentiles, to open eyes that are blind, to free the captives from prison, and to release from the dungeon those who sit in darkness. I am the Lord; that is my Name! I will not give my glory to another or my praise to idols."*

Many people mistakenly think that God chose Israel because "Jews are very smart and know how to make money. He chose the Jews because they are good doctors and lawyers. He chose the Jews because they have Nobel Prizes." Some Jews think that we are better than everybody else too, but this is not correct.

In fact, the Bible reveals to us why God chose the Jews. He chose Israel to be a light to the nations, to open the eyes of the blind, and to release the captives. When He came to Abraham in Northern Syria, He told him to leave his father and mother and to go to the land that He would show him. Then He gave him three promises: the promise of the Land, the promise of the seed, and the promise of the blessing for all the families of the earth. That is why God chose Abraham and his seed forever. There is no other promise in all the Scriptures which appears so many times as the promise that God made to Abraham, Isaac, Jacob, and the seed of Israel. The promise of the multiplication of the seed, the promise of being a blessing to all the nations of the earth, and the promise that He would give the land of Canaan to Israel and to their seed forever, appears in Genesis twenty times.

The Church has tried to appropriate the promise of the seed and the promise of the blessing for themselves. They do not want to appropriate the promise of the Land very much these days because land is concrete and real. It is hard to spiritualize land, so they say, "Well, that was in the Old Testament, for the Jews, but now that we are in the New Testament era, the land is not important." Ironically, the Catholic Church owns fifteen percent of the prime land in Israel, and the Greek Orthodox

Church owns huge portions of Jerusalem, including the land on which the Knesset stands. If the land is so unimportant to them, I wish they would give it to us! They appropriated all this land back in the time of the Crusades when the Church decided they did care about acquiring the promise of the Holy Land and sent their armies to conquer it, but military might alone does not decide true ownership in the eyes of God. Deuteronomy 32:8 says that God decided and divided up lands and borders long ago according to his own criteria and not according to our own sense of entitlement, nationalism, or demographic needs. God made physical promises to Israel, and all of those physical promises remain with the Jewish people even to this day, whether or not the Church or the nations want to acknowledge it.

It is a package deal; God chose Israel when He chose Abraham. Israel's election did not come from the covenant He made with them at Sinai, but rather when God chose Abraham. God had to choose Abraham to ensure that the world was not buried in the darkness of idolatry. God chose Abraham in chapter 12 of Genesis immediately after Genesis 11 recounts humanity's rebellion against God at the Tower of Babel. The only time that human beings united was to rebel against God and build the Tower of Babel, so God divided the nations before they could do any more damage to the world. Before the Tower of Babel, there were no nations, and there were no Gentiles. Everybody spoke the same language, and they were all cousins, the descendants of Noah and his children. God only divided them into nations when they united against Him and wanted to build a tower to be free from the power of God and his influence on them. There were no nations before that, and there was no idolatry before that. There is no mention of idols before or after Noah until the Tower of Babel. Idolatry and multiple languages entered the world after the Tower of Babel, and Abraham was chosen after the Tower of Babel to ensure that this rebellion of humanity against God would be fixed.

In Hebrew we call this concept *Tikkun Olam*—that the world rebelled against God and, therefore, has to be fixed. It was damaged and has to be repaired, so God chose Abraham in order to repair the world and to restore humanity back to faith in the One God, the creator of the heavens and the earth. That is why God chose Israel, and that is why Yeshua the Messiah was born a Jew. He could have been born to any nation in the world that God chose, but he was born a Jew from the seed of David, from the seed of Abraham, because of God's mission for Israel. It was not an accident, and He was not chosen by a lottery. God designed it that way before the creation of the world because He knew what was going to happen in history before it began. Election has to do with this task of bringing the nations back to the knowledge and worship of the One God. It was not because of Jewish pride or Jewish abilities, but rather because God wanted to take a person with faith, Abraham, give him a seed that is supernatural, and use that seed in the history of mankind to bring the nations back to Himself, since God loved the entire world, not only the Jews.

A lot of people who are not Jewish resist this concept and say, "What right do the Jews have to be chosen? Are they better than we are?" They somehow get the idea that being chosen is a wonderful, exclusive thing. In this regard, I have to agree with Tevye in *Fiddler on the Roof* though and say, "Why can't God choose somebody else for a change? We have suffered enough." Being chosen brings not only laughs and good times. Our greatest suffering as a nation, in fact, was at the hands of those who called themselves Christians, although anti-Semitism also has a pagan basis.

God loves the world because He created it, and even though both Jews and Gentiles were rebellious, God wanted to bring his children back. Just like the father of the Prodigal Son was waiting for his son to come home, God never gave up on his children. God loves his children and is waiting to open up the house for them, to give them robes, to kill the fatted calf, to put rings on their fingers, and say, "Welcome home, children." He is waiting for both the prodigal Jews and the prodigal Gentiles to repent and come back to Him.

Israel's role in history has nothing to do with personal salvation. It has to do with a task for which God chose Israel in the beginning, to be a light to the nations, so those who are walking in darkness can see the light of God. Even in the darkest hours of history, the worst anti-Semites in the world, including the Nazis, knew that. At the turn of the Twentieth Century, the Czar asked Rasputin (a horribly immoral and anti-Semitic Russian Orthodox priest) to prove that God existed. Even though Rasputin hated Jews, his response to the Czar was: "I'll answer you with one word: Israel." God's interaction with Israel is undeniable proof of his existence and his insistence on righteous behavior from his children.

Anyone who wants proof that God exists should just look at the history of the Jewish people. We have survived against all odds because God wanted us to survive. In most of our history, even most Jews did not want to be Jews. We did everything to assimilate, but God did not let it happen. Every time we wanted to assimilate, He sent the enemy, whether it was the Romans, Greeks, Germans, Russians, or Ukrainians to remind us of our true calling and identity. Many Jews tragically only returned to God and their Jewish identity through the fires of persecution, but He will not let us go.

In the 1920s, the Jews in Germany said, "By religion we are Jews, but our nationality is German. We are first Germans and then Jews." It was not very many years later that God reminded them of the truth. According to Hitler, even a person with only one Jewish grandparent was Jewish enough to be sent to a concentration camp and murdered in gas chambers. All these horrible things he did reminded us again that we are Jews, that we are the seed of Abraham and that we have a task in history. That job is not finished yet, and that is why God has kept us alive in spite of our enemies and even in spite of ourselves. Israel's task did not end with bringing the Messiah into the world in the First Century, and what happens to the Jews still affects every corner of the earth. Israel is still supposed to be a light to the nations, to show the truth of the one God, to demonstrate moral behavior, and to bring God glory throughout the earth. That job will not be finished until the Messiah comes back to Zion.

Why did He choose the Jews and not somebody else? Deuteronomy 7:6-8 says, *"For you are a people holy to the Lord your God. The Lord has chosen you out of all the peoples on the face of the earth to be his people, his treasured possession. The Lord did not set his affection on you and choose you because you were more numerous than other peoples, for you were the fewest of all peoples. But it was because the Lord loved you and kept the oath he swore to your forefathers that he brought you out with a mighty hand and redeemed you from the land of slavery, from the power of Pharaoh, King of Egypt."* God chose the Jews because they were the least of all the nations.

If He had chosen the Egyptians, they would have said, "Of course, because we are the smartest nation with the best engineers and the most talented builders." If He had chosen the Babylonians they could have said, "He chose us because we are a great empire with the biggest armies. We have ruled all the way from the steppes of Asia to the Adriatic Sea. We have the biggest rivers in the Middle East and the most ancient culture with the first written language of humanity." Instead, God chose the least of all the nations, the smallest nation of the ancient world, so that nobody could boast and say, "He chose us because of how great we are."

He chose us for the sake of the Gentiles, not for our own sake. We have paid a very high price for being the chosen people, but our Jewish Messiah has been a blessing to the entire world. The sign above the cross said, "Yeshua of Nazareth, King of the Jews." Christians today enter their church buildings to worship a Jewish savior, and no one can take the Jew out of Yeshua. He was a Jew when He lived in Israel, He worshipped as a Jew, He went to the synagogue, and He went to the Temple in Jerusalem just like the other Jews of his time. He loved the Torah and God's commandments, and He lived perfectly under the Law. He died as the king of the Jews, and no matter how much a person tries to spiritualize Him, He will always remain a Jew. We worship a Jewish savior, and a Jew shed his blood for our transgressions, as the Prophets of Israel predicted about Him thousands of years before He was born. No one can deny that, no matter how much they hate Jews or deny Israel's right to exist.

Paul says that the Gentiles need to know into what they were grafted and into whom they were joined. Paul says in Ephesians 2:12, *"Therefore remember that formerly you who are Gentiles by birth and called 'uncircumcised...'"* There are no Gentiles in the Church. A person can be a Gentile "formerly" before they believed in God and accepted his covenants. Someone could be a Gentile before being blessed by the promises and entering the commonwealth of Israel, before having his sins forgiven, and before being buried with Yeshua the Messiah and being raised into the newness of life in baptism. Once someone starts to follow Yeshua the Messiah, however, he is a child of Abraham.

Non-Jews who believe in Yeshua become fellow citizens with God's people and members of God's household. The children of Abraham receive the covenants, the promises, the God of Israel, and the Scriptures of Israel. One confusing statement here that needs clarification is the phrase that says, *"Abolishing in his flesh the Law with its commandments and regulations."* Too many people read this verse incorrectly and think that Yeshua abolished the Old Covenant, that is, the covenant with the Jews through Abraham or even the covenant of the Mosaic Law. The continued validity of the Mosaic covenant is a discussion for another book entirely, but we are focusing here on the Abrahamic covenant through which the Jews became God's people and into which the Church was grafted. When Yeshua died, and his blood was shed, a New Covenant came into effect. The source for this New Covenant, Jeremiah 31:31, makes it clear that this New Covenant was not with the Church. According to Jeremiah, God promised to make this New Covenant with the House of Israel and the House of Judah.

Yeshua says several times in the Gospels, *"I came for the lost sheep of the House of Israel."* Only after his resurrection did He tell his disciples, *"Go and make disciples of all nations… teaching them to obey everything I have commanded you."*[1] Mark 16:15-16 says, *"Go into all the world and preach the Good News to all creation. Whoever believes and is baptized*

---

1   Matt 28:19-20

will be saved, but whoever does not believe will be condemned."
The New Testament never teaches people to kneel down at an altar and repeat a prayer in order to be saved. God's people anywhere are my brothers and sisters, and God did not tell anybody to join a church. He said in Acts 2:47, *"And the Lord added to their number those who were being saved"* but never mentioned anything about becoming members of a church.

Israel was called for the sake of the world, and Israel's election was for the sake of the Gentiles. It is hard to believe, but even Israel's rejection of Yeshua was for the sake of the world. Romans 11:7 says, *"What then? What Israel sought so earnestly it did not obtain, but the elect did."* This is not talking about the Church but about the elect of Israel, the remnant he mentioned in the previous verses. Some of the Jews accepted and were elected, while the others were hardened. Continuing from verses 8-11, *"As it is written: 'God gave them a spirit of stupor, eyes so that they could not see, and ears so that they could not hear, to this very day.' And David says: 'May their table become a snare and a trap, a stumbling block and a retribution for them. May their eyes be darkened so they cannot see and their backs be bent forever.' Again I ask, 'Did they stumble so as to fall beyond recovery?' Not at all! Rather because of their transgression, salvation has come to the Gentiles to make Israel envious."* That is revelation from Paul. Salvation came to the Gentiles, according to Paul, because the Jews stumbled, so that the Church may make Israel envious. Then verse 12 promises, *"But if their transgression means riches for the world, and their loss means riches for the Gentiles, how much greater riches will their fullness bring!"*

God says that He gave the Jews a spirit of blindness so the Gentiles can come in. Then Paul asks the question in verse 12, *"Did God cause them to stumble so as to never rise up again, so that they may never recover?"* Paul's answer is, *"Not at all!"* They will recover. In the same chapter, in Romans 11:25-26, Paul says, *"I do not want you to be ignorant of this mystery, brothers, so that you may not be conceited. Israel has experienced a hardening in part until the full number of the Gentiles has come in. And so all Israel will be saved."* The Jews are going to be saved, and they will accept Yeshua as their Messiah when He reveals Himself truly to them sometime in the future.

Romans 11:28 continues, *"As far as the Gospel is concerned, they are enemies on your account; but as far as election is concerned they are loved on account of the Patriarchs,"* [meaning Abraham, Isaac, Jacob, Joseph, Moses, and all the Patriarchs of our faith]. He says clearly that they are still the elect people of God because their election did not come due to their obedience. Election came as a result of God's promise to Abraham, Isaac, Jacob, and Moses.

Israel is still the beloved people of God because of the Patriarchs. That is Israel's condition for faith, and that is why we need to preach the Gospel to them. No nation has been promised salvation, except the nation of Israel. God saves many people from many other nations out of his mercy, but He has no obligation to do so because He only gave a promise to Israel. The Gospel will flourish eventually. The seed we sow will produce fruit because we are preaching to people who have a promise of God, *"Thus all Israel shall be saved."*

Israel is still the elect people of God, and the Church has a direct and eternal relationship with Israel. Too many of its members have been robbed of the essence of that relationship by the traditions of men who twisted the Word of God and separated the Church from its roots. It is time for the Church to repent and say to the Jews along with Ruth, *"Your people*

*will be my people. Your God will be my God. Wherever you go
I will follow!"*

Chapter Three:

The Church

We started our journey by talking about God and the importance of his unity. These things do not sink in immediately because it takes time to digest the importance of the oneness of God, who is the Father of us all. Next we saw that God elected Israel for the sake of the whole world so they could be a light to all the nations of the world. The blessing that God gave Abraham and his seed forever is that all the families of the earth would be blessed by Abraham and his seed. In Acts 10 Peter tells Cornelius, the first Gentile to hear the Gospel, *"God is no respecter of persons, but in every nation anyone who fears him and does what is right is acceptable to him."*

The Church is mentioned only one time in the four Gospels, in Matthew 16:16-18 after Peter made the confession, *"You are the Messiah, the son of the living God."* Yeshua turned to him and said, *"Blessed are you Simon Bar Jonah, for this was not revealed to you by man, but by my Father in heaven. And I tell you that you are Peter, and upon this rock I will build my church..."* That is the only time in all four Gospels that the word *ekklesia* "Church" is mentioned, so it is unique. Yeshua did not speak much about the Church. All through the Gospels, He taught the twelve disciples and the Jewish crowds who followed Him, but He did not teach them about the Church. The Greek word *ekklesia* only begins to be popular in the book of Acts, where it is mentioned dozens of times and then in Paul's letters to refer to the Church.

On the other hand, the word "disciples" is mentioned dozens of times in the Gospels, but after Acts 21, the word "disciple," does not appear in the New Testament. In other words, Yeshua spent his time on earth with his disciples, whom He taught and with whom He had a relationship. He fed thousands of people but had a relationship only with his disciples. Then that relationship shifted from a small group of Jews who followed Him in the hills of Galilee and Judea to become a larger community, *ekklesia.*

English Bibles never use the term "church" in the Old Testament, but they tend to use "solemn assembly" for the Hebrew words that mean the same thing as *ekklesia* in Greek. Checking a Greek concordance for the word *ekklesia* in the Septuagint (the ancient Greek translation of the Old Testament) leads to an interesting discovery. *Ekklesia,* the exact Greek word that is translated as "church" in the New Testament, appears hundreds of times in the Greek Old Testament to translate two Hebrew words: *kahal* "the crowd, the community," and *ha-edah[1]* "the crowd, the assembly, the community."

This is the essence of the Church. The Church is a community and a group of people, not a building, an organization, a board of directors, or a creed. We have incorrectly adopted the European model of the Church, in which it is the institution, the building, or the organization. Never in the Bible is the word "church" or *ekklesia* used in the sense of an organization. It is always the people themselves. The Church can meet anywhere, and in Acts the Church met from house to house daily, not only on Sundays or Wednesday nights. Acts says that the Church met regularly in public places like in the School of Tyranus or in the courts of the Temple in

---

1   Edah in Hebrew also means witness.

Jerusalem. The Church is the people who follow Yeshua, no matter where they happen to be.

Contrary to the impression of most of today's believers, the Bible never says that the Church was born at Pentecost (Shavuot) in Acts 2. If the Church was born at Pentecost, it was a Church made only of Jews because the first Gentile believer was Cornelius in Acts 10. The 3,000 that were pricked in their hearts by the words of Peter and said, "What shall we do?" were all either born Jews or converts to Judaism, who came from Pontus, Libya, Rome, Arabia, Egypt, and other places in the Jewish Diaspora. Many people have the mistaken impression that they were not Jews, since they came from abroad, from all over the Roman Empire, to worship in Jerusalem. They were all Jews, however, so any Church born at Pentecost was only a Jewish one.

What really happened at Pentecost was not totally unexpected, and it was not a surprise that a new body was born. God's prophets predicted it seven or eight hundred years before Yeshua was born. The Church was the fulfillment of Israel's expectations and one continuation of God's people. The Church was what God had prepared from the very beginning of his relationship with Abraham and his seed. It was not a new invention that landed from Mars. When Peter was asked, "What is going on here?" he replied, "This is what the prophet Joel predicted." Joel was one of the prophets of Israel from the Old Testament that lived in the Seventh Century BCE, so the Church was clearly in the plan of God for many years before it ever happened. However, let us not confuse God's plan to create the Church with any idea of replacement or rejection of Israel.

Many people believe that Gentiles entered the plan of God because the Jews were unfaithful. The Church has taught that God got tired of the Jews and took the second best, the Gentiles. The Prophets prove this is not true though, just as in Jonah, God had prepared a way for the Gentiles to leave their idols, darkness, witchcraft, and immorality behind and to come to the knowledge of God Almighty, the God of Abraham, Isaac, and Jacob.

The Eighth Century prophet Isaiah is the one who originally said, *"My house will be called a house of prayer for all the nations."* Isaiah 66 even predicts that the Gentiles will serve as priests in the Temple of God. In Isaiah 56:6-7 it reads, *"Also the foreigners who join themselves to the Lord, to minister to him and to love the name of the Lord, to be his servants, everyone who keeps from profaning the Sabbath and holds fast to my covenant, even those I will bring to my holy mountain and make them joyful in my house of prayer. Their burnt offerings and their sacrifices will be acceptable on my altar, for my house will be called a house of prayer for all the peoples."* That astonishing statement is in the Old Testament, so it is not Christian invention designed to replace the Jews. In the end of days, these non-Jewish priests will be equal to the Jewish ones in God's sight because it is impossible for God to have second class children. They do not replace the Jews, but rather join with them.

In the book of Acts, before Paul went out of the church of Antioch, the elders of that church anointed him and commissioned him to go preach the gospel. They said that they were anointing him to take the gospel of Yeshua the Messiah to the Gentiles. That was the mission to which he had been called. He did not go to the Gentiles because the Jews rejected him. He went to the Gentiles because God called him to be the apostle to the Gentiles. The Church is the fulfillment of God's expectations for Israel in her mission to be a light to the world. The Church is also the fulfillment and the continuation of God's expectations for humanity and his children forever. This work is not yet finished, however.

God never intended to leave any nation or people out of his love. He always loved the whole world, even though some of us and our nations rebelled against Him and chose to worship idols. We chose in our rebellious hearts to reject the Almighty God of Israel and to worship demons. Many people think that idols are little statues, but the statues are just the symbols of the idols. The New Testament declares in 1 Corinthians 10:20, *"The sacrifices of pagans are offered to demons, not to God...,"* quoting Deuteronomy 32:17-21. People chose to worship idols, even though they were not obligated or even encouraged to do so. Even the Jews, who were supposed to know God, sometimes slipped, fell away, and chose to worship idols, which is why God punished them with the destruction of the First Temple and the First Exile. God is a wonderful God of love who wants his children to be happy, rich, prosperous, healthy, and good. If they sin and choose to rebel and be disobedient, however, He wants his children to be educated. Some of the trials we are suffering are for our education. Whoever does not learn from the book has to learn from experience, but it is much more expensive to learn from experience than it is to learn from books.

The Church is not an afterthought. It is a part of the original plan of God from the very beginning. Jeremiah, the Psalms, and the Torah itself also teach that God never intended to only choose one nation and to abandon the rest of humanity. The Church is part of God's original plan, and it is supposed to be a community and a family. In the New Testament, the Church is the community and the people, not the establishment. It is the proletariat, the people themselves, because Yeshua did not die for an institution or for a board of directors. Yeshua died for all of humanity, for the simple and the poor, because He wanted to lift us up. Paul says in 2 Corinthians 8:9, *"For you know of the grace of our Lord Yeshua the Messiah, that though he was rich, yet for your sakes he became poor, so that you through his poverty might become rich."*

One more thing the New Testament teaches about the Church is that it can have many names. The New Testament gives many options because nobody has a monopoly on the Church of God. One term the New Testament uses to refer to it more than twenty times is "the Way." This is why our organization in Israel is called, *Netivyah*, the way of the Lord. We took it from Acts 24:14, where Paul says, *"I belong to that which is called the Way."*

Even to the very end of his life, Paul never once said, "I was a Jew, and then I became a Christian. I did belong to Israel, and now I belong to the Seventh Day Adventists or the Jehovah's Witnesses" or to any one of the many denominations that exist today. Paul, Peter, Ya'akov [James], and all the apostles remained Jews. The early church in Jerusalem was the head of the worldwide Church, and all the other congregations knew they were following the Jewish leaders and the Jewish Messiah.

The Church is really a fulfillment of Israel's expectation, not a replacement of Israel. Those who believe in Yeshua are not grafted into Rome or into Martin Luther, but rather to the Olive Tree, which is natural. Those who believe are joined with Israel and become a part of the commonwealth of Israel according to Ephesians 2:12. God has promised that his people will be winners and not losers, lenders and not borrowers, if they will just obey Him. The people of Israel are the only people God has ever had. There are no more Gentiles in the kingdom of God. All those who believe become the children of Abraham and join with Israel. They do not replace Israel, but rather become partakers of the same holy food that God fed Israel in the Spirit of God for thousands of years. It is true that those who follow Yeshua are under the New Covenant, but the New Covenant was made with the House of Judah and with the House of Israel. It does not belong to the Church; it belongs to Israel. Jeremiah the prophet predicted the New Covenant, and no one under the New Covenant can ignore his relationship with Israel.

In summary, the Church and Israel are the right and left hands of the will of God. They are not opposite institutions, which are at war with one another or competing with one another. They do not have separate constitutions or separate Words of God. The Church and Israel together constitute the people of God. Just as in Israel there is a remnant walking in the light, there is also such a remnant in the Church. There always was a remnant walking in the light, but the majority never walked in the light or obeyed God's will. The majority was that which cried out to Moses, "Take us back to Egypt! We miss the cucumbers, the onions, and the garlic!" The majority worshipped idols or followed the Pope instead of the Word of God.

Of course, there were always the 'Calebs' and the 'Joshuas' who said, "Lord, we cannot do it because there are giants in the land, but we can go in and take it with your name, your power, and your spirit. If you go in front of us and fight our battles, like you promised, we can do it, Lord." The problem is that the majority always stood by and whined, "We have no chance. Oh Lord, where have you brought us? Look at all these negative things. Half of our congregation is poor, the other half is confused, and the other half is incompetent." What the majority forgets is that the Lord can use anyone He wants; He can take a shepherd and put a crown on his head.

Think of the contrast between King David and King Saul, who was a great warrior and a very tall man. When they crowned King Saul, he was head and shoulders taller than all the men of Israel, and he was also a handsome man. He was a warrior, but when Goliath marched up the valley, stood in front of the people of Israel and said, "Send me one of your warriors to fight against me," all the great men of Israel, including King Saul, were shaking in their boots, even though they were trained men of war. Then David entered, a young boy who was being disobedient to his father. His father sent him to bring food to his brothers and a little bribe to the generals and told him to stay out of trouble. Yet David could not stand to see the name of the God of Israel being abused and misused and the army of Israel full of fear. He decided to do something about it himself and not let this uncircumcised Philistine revile the name of the God of Israel. He went with nothing but a slingshot in his hands and won the battle, not because he was so strong or so smart, but because he was fighting for a just, honest, and godly cause. He won the battle because he did it with God's tools and not with the tools of the world. The obedience of one boy won the battle for Israel, despite the fear and lack of faith of the majority.

It is a big challenge for believers today to fight with God's tools. Many congregations want to win the war with the tools of the world, with the sword of Goliath, the Hollywood presentation, and the cardboard façade, but God has always had the real thing. The real thing is always a lot harder, heavier, and more difficult than the pretend, the fake, and the imitation. We tend to judge our effectiveness by the number of people sitting in our pews, signatures on a doctrinal statement, or the amount of money collected in the offering plate instead of by God's standards of faithfulness and good deeds, which are harder to measure. We do not like to welcome the poor, the homeless, the not well-dressed, the emotionally needy, and the crazy people of the world into our churches because they do not present the sort of image we want to convey.

The Church is a community, a family, and one of the wonderful things about families is that we do not choose our children in a shop window. Neither do we choose our brothers and sisters in the marketplace. Whomever God gives us as brothers and sisters, children, and parents is whom we have for the rest of their lives. Sometimes dysfunctional children are born into the family of God, but they are my brothers and sisters, so I love them. Although I did not choose them, I love them because God gave them eternal life and filled them with his Spirit, and now we are family. The Church is all about this unconditional love. It is not about people with well-combed hair and shiny new suits; it is about people who were sinners but who have been redeemed by the blood of Yeshua. They have been grafted in and have become a part of the people of God, a part of the commonwealth of Israel, a part of a long line of remnant people who stayed faithful when everybody else walked away. The Church is not a replacement of Israel; it is the continuation of Israel's mission.

When God promised Abraham those wonderful promises, He said, "Your seed will be as many as the sand on the seashore, as many as the stars of the heavens, beyond the ability to count them" (Genesis 13:16, 15:5). I recently saw a calculation in an Israeli newspaper saying that if at the time of the Exodus from Egypt there were 600,000 Jewish men between the ages of twenty and fifty (men of war), we would have reached more than a billion people with natural multiplication if we were a normal nation. The fact is, however, that there are only fourteen to sixteen million Jews in the whole world. The anti-Semitic persecutions of the world have taken their toll on the Jewish population. So where is the promise that God gave to Abraham? Where are all the stars of the heavens and the sand of the sea?

The answer lies in comparing the words God spoke to Abraham to the words that God speaks to the Church in Revelation 7:9-10, which is actually an allusion to God's words to Abraham in Genesis. *"After this I looked, and there before me was a great multitude that no one could count from every nation, tribe, people, and language, standing before the throne, and in front of the Lamb. They were wearing white robes and were holding palm branches in their hands. And they cried out in a loud voice, 'Salvation belongs to our God who sits on the throne and to the Lamb!'"*

Notice the words, *"A great multitude that no one could count."* These are the words and the promises that God gave Abraham, and that great multitude according to Revelation includes people from every nation, tribe and color. These words here in Revelation allude to God's promise to Abraham in Genesis 22 after Abraham nearly sacrificed Isaac. This means that God's promises did not fall on unfruitful ground and that his promises are being fulfilled right now. Every time a soul gets saved, it is added to the seed of Abraham by faith. God's Church is connected with Israel inseparably. Anyone who worships the God of Abraham, Isaac, and Jacob in the name of Yeshua the Messiah is connected to the people of God, the people of Israel, the root of Jesse, and the seed of Abraham. The Church that God established is one Church with one Lord, one spirit, one head, one baptism, and one people of God— not replacing Israel but joining with Israel.

Christian theology has traditionally said that the Jews have rejected Yeshua, so God has rejected them. It is true that the majority of the Jews rejected Yeshua in his day and that the majority of the Jews continue to reject Him. The fact is, however, that God is saving their seats, and they have a "reserved" sign. He is waiting for them to come home, and they are coming home all over the world.

The ultimate event in the end-times fulfillment of prophecy is the return of the Gospel back to where it started in Jerusalem. May the Lord use us all with our incompetence, with our shortcomings, with our mistakes, and with our failures, but use us to see the Gospel preached, the kingdom of God breaking forth, and the multiplication of God's blessing upon the world and upon all of Israel!

Chapter Four:

Yeshua and the Pharisees

One of the greatest mistakes of Church history is the way it has typically related to the Pharisees. This Second Temple Period group frequently appears in the pages of the New Testament in a negative context, or conflict over spiritual and *halachic[1]* questions, some of which Yeshua rebukes them for, and others of which He defends. This picture seems to place Yeshua on one side of the border and the Pharisees on the other, which rooted a negative opinion of the Pharisees as the worst enemies of the Messiah in Christian tranidtion. This negative worldview also greatly influenced the Church's way of relating to Jewish tradition, which was considered to be the extension of the Pharisaic tradition. The false dichotomy the Church created between the spiritual worlds of Yeshua and the Pharisees made it seem as though they were total opposites and strangers to one another. This conclusion is completely detached from historical reality and could not be further from the truth. The Pharisees were considered to be the most faithful to the Torah, which is precisely why Yeshua criticized them when they did evil in the name of "religious piety."

In order to understand the things that Yeshua said to the Pharisees, we must first properly understand their place within the wide variety of sects and groups of Judaism in the Second Temple Period. At that time the Jews lived under Roman occupation and the client-kingship of the family of Herod the

---

[1] *Halacha* - From the Hebrew word for "walking," traditional guidelines for practical daily life accepted by observant Jews.

Idumean, who had converted to Judaism. There were many different sectarian groups of Jews in those days, some of which we know more about than others. The Sadducees were one group which we know about primarily from Josephus Flavius, the New Testament, and a few Rabbinic sources. Many of them belonged to the ruling aristocracy and were the descendants of the Hasmonean family who had ruled Judea in the Maccabean period. Although ostensibly revolting against Hellenism, the Hasmonean kings eventually became very Hellenized in culture, though they tried to remain relatively strict in religious matters, especially those that related to the Temple. They were not a large group, but they had tremendous influence because of their wealth and political power and since they controlled the Jerusalem Temple. One learns from both the New Testament and Josephus that they did not believe in life after death or any form of resurrection, a belief that caused them to take a pragmatic approach to religious rules whenever they conflicted with the dictates of the foreign government. They also did not respect the concept of the Oral Law and the work of the sages in establishing *halacha*. They rarely believed in miracles and continued revelation of any sort. From what we can read in literary sources from the time period, it seems that the Pharisees and Sadducees were nearly in constant conflict with one another.

There were also more radical groups of eschatologically conscious sectarian Jews, such as the Essenes. Some of them were so convinced of the impurity of the Jerusalem Temple and the Herodian government that they withdrew into the Judean desert to live an ascetic, proto-monastic lifestyle while they studied and interpreted their holy books and planned for the final eschatological battle between the Sons of Light (themselves) and the Sons of Darkness (everyone else). They considered themselves to be the righteous remnant who would survive to the coming of the Messiah and who would merit to rule Israel and serve in its Temple (many of them were priests) in the Messianic Age. We know nothing about these groups from the New Testament, although we know a little about them from Josephus and Philo of Alexandria. Most importantly, the discovery of the Dead Sea Scrolls, many of which were written by and for Essene-like sectarians, opened up hundreds of fascinating sources about their lives and beliefs to scholars.

Another group, whom Josephus calls "the Fourth Philosophy," consisted of the Zealots, Jews who swore to break the yoke of foreign rule from over themselves at any cost because they thought it was forbidden for Jews to be ruled by pagans. Some of these Zealots became brigands who formed bands of guerilla-robbers and assassination squads who targeted with equal ferocity the Romans and any wealthy or powerful Jews, whom they viewed as collaborators. It was the Zealots who eventually succeeded in winning over much of the Jewish population to their cause by default when they began the First Jewish Revolt against the Romans in 66 CE, but most of them were killed in the horrific battles of the war. A few survived long enough to launch the Second Jewish Revolt in 135 CE, but after it was quashed, this Jewish sect perished completely, never to rise again.

The Pharisees, about whom we read in Josephus and the New Testament, were a group of Jewish religious leaders who tried to apply the Torah to every matter of daily life and therefore spent much of their time developing *halacha* (the way to walk in daily life), which consisted of oral traditions on how to put the written Torah into practical usage. The question of their relationship to the rabbis or sages of later Rabbinic literature is a complex one, especially since the only ancient Jews who were willing to write about themselves publicly as "Pharisees" were Josephus and Paul the Apostle. It used to be commonly thought that the Pharisees just changed their name to "the Rabbis" after the destruction of the Temple, but more recent scholarship sees more shades of gray on this question. One possibility is that there was a small group of Pharisees who were rabbis and who survived the Temple's destruction through the deal their leader Yochanan ben Zakai made with the Roman conquerors. Since most of the other groups perished in the Revolt, this small group of Rabbi-Pharisees gradually grew in popularity and power and eventually won over the common people to their cause after several centuries of struggle. They emphasized religious education for every Jew. Because of their belief in the Resurrection and the reward of the faithful in the world to come, they urged following the Torah at almost any cost to purse, property, or body.

The religious persuasion of the ordinary people in the time of Yeshua is also difficult to discover, since they did not write books describing their religious beliefs and practices. Some Rabbinic sources speak derisively of the ignorance and impiety of the "people of the land" and demand that the truly religious Jew separate himself from them, their homes, and their food. It seems that the masses of these members of "Common Judaism" (if there was such a thing) were primarily devoted to their service to the one God of Israel, the Torah of Israel, and the Temple of Israel, although sometimes the finer points of *halacha* were lost on them. They were primarily farmers, craftsmen, and minor merchants who lived in small towns and villages and were not wealthy or powerful. These were the masses that so eagerly followed Yeshua and admired his profound religious teachings that focused on the intent of the heart, along with Torah observance and their everyday concerns. His care for them in providing them food, healing, and teaching drew them to follow Him all over the country to hear Him teach and to be healed from their various diseases.

Yeshua and his disciples (and Paul) had a completely Pharisaic worldview, as one sees from Paul's behavior before the Sanhedrin in Acts 23:6-9. *"Then Paul, knowing that some of them were Sadducees and the others Pharisees, called out in the Sanhedrin, 'My brothers, I am a Pharisee, the son of a Pharisee. I stand on trial because of my hope in the resurrection of the dead.' When he said this a dispute broke out between the Pharisees and the Sadducees, and the assembly was divided. (The Sadducees say that there is no resurrection, and that there are neither angels nor spirits, but the Pharisees acknowledge them all). There was a great uproar, and some of the teachers of the law who were Pharisees stood up and argued vigorously. 'We find nothing wrong with this man,' they said. 'What if a spirit or an angel has spoken to him?'"*

In this passage Luke adds notes about the disputes between the Pharisees and the Sadducees in order to explain the Pharisees' support for Paul. On most of the points of conflict between the Pharisees and the Sadducees, such as the resurrection, belief in miracles, and continued revelation through the Holy Spirit, the New Testament takes a completely Pharisaic point of view, rather than one that follows the Sadducees.

The Gospels also present the picture that Yeshua and his disciples maintained close societal connections and relationships with groups of Pharisees. These accounts from Luke evidence this fact. *"And one of the Pharisees invited Him [Yeshua] to eat with him, so He went into the Pharisee's house and reclined at the table."*[1] *"One Sabbath, when Yeshua went to eat at the house of a prominent Pharisee, He was being carefully watched."*[2] These stories show that Yeshua routinely associated with Pharisees and trusted their standards of purity and kosher food and dishes. This concept is important to remember when examining the story in which He criticizes the Pharisees' meal practices as being too strict. Yeshua Himself was careful to observe the *halachic* norms of the Pharisees, although some of the passages that record their arguments make Yeshua appear to be breaking the Torah. He clearly refutes this charge in his famous statement in Matthew 5:17-20, however, *"Do not think that I have come to abolish the Law and the Prophets; I have not come to abolish them but to fulfill them. I tell you the truth, until heaven and earth disappear, not the smallest letter, not the least stroke of a pen will by any means disappear from the Law until everything is accomplished. Anyone who breaks the least one of these commandments and teaches others to do the same will be called least in the kingdom of heaven, but whoever practices and teaches these commands will be called great in the kingdom of heaven. For I tell you that unless your righteousness surpasses that of the Pharisees and the teachers of the Law, you will certainly not enter the kingdom of heaven."* These are strong words in favor of the eternity of the Torah.

For all those who doubt these words and are thinking about all the occasions where Yeshua and the Pharisees debate and seem to oppose each other, we will now take a closer look at some New Testament passages in order to clarify our understanding and interpretation of them. Many of them reflect a type of internal Jewish religious dispute that had been going

1   Luke 7:36

2   Luke 14:1

on for thousands of years and, in fact, still continues unto this day. Many of the most controversial statements against the Pharisees appear in the pages of the Gospel of Matthew, leading some people to label this book as anti-Semitic. It is true that the misinterpretation of Matthew's words has brought a lot of horrible violence against the Jewish people over the centuries and a great fear of reading it. Nevertheless, all this harsh-sounding rhetoric actually forms a key element in the quest of New Testament scholars to identify Matthew's intended audience. There is a trend in some of today's New Testament scholarship to view Matthew as the product of a group of believing Jews who were still Pharisaic in their *halacha* and way of life. By this argument, the strong critiques of the Pharisees and other Jewish religious leaders are merely part of an internal dispute in which people were much harder on each other because of their common background and training than they would have been on any outsider of whom they did not expect so much.

The first and most infamous of the incidents we will examine here occurs in Matthew 15:1-2, which says, *"Then some Pharisees and scribes came to Yeshua from Jerusalem saying, 'Why do your disciples break the traditional teaching of the elders? They do not wash their hands before they eat bread.'"* Since man was created in the image of God, he also has the character trait of loving to create things. Although this sounds like a good thing, this advantage that humans have over animals also has a problematic side. Sometimes when we humans create and invent new ideas or developments, we get so passionate about our achievements (and mistakes) that we forget that we are not God. We tend to develop the false mentality that someone has appointed us to preserve God's order on the earth and to think that we have the right or even the obligation to interfere in the lives of others and to judge their deeds, to the most severe standard, although we judge ourselves by the lightest standard. This is exactly the mistake the Pharisees who were criticizing Yeshua in this passage were making. We do have a duty to correct each other in love, but our motives must be pure and right when we do so, something which is rare.

The focus of the passage is not whether it is right or wrong to wash hands before eating bread, which was a common *halachic* debate that still had not been settled in the time of Yeshua. Yeshua did not criticize the tradition of washing hands or even the concept of the tradition of the elders in general. It appears in the passage that He Himself washed his hands before eating, since the charge is directed against his disciples and not Him. Nothing here says that washing hands before eating bread (*netilat yadayim*) is wrong; it simply says that it is not a commandment in the Torah, but rather a **custom** developed from the Torah's rules about priests washing in the Tabernacle. Yeshua criticizes these Pharisees for being extremely strict about matters that are mere **customs,** while ignoring clear and important commandments from the written Torah, which we can be absolutely certain are God's will.

Judaism differentiates between commandments that are *de'Oraita* (from the written Torah and thus absolutely from God) and commandments that are *de'Rabbanan* (given by the sages). Since the sages' authority to establish *halacha* is supposed to come from Moses and God, both types of commandments are binding. Nevertheless, the punishment for breaking a *de'Oraita* commandment is much more severe than for breaking one established by the rabbis. The commandments derived from the written Torah are also considered more important most of the time, so not all commandments are "created equal." Which commandments are the most important or take precedence over others are matters of constant discussion between Yeshua and the Pharisees in the Gospels, especially on questions of carrying out acts of compassion, such as healing or picking grain to eat if a person was hungry on the Sabbath. Many of the final settlements of these *halachic* controversies were not fully established until the time of the finishing of the Talmud, centuries after Yeshua, with some of the opinions coming down on his side and others on the side of the Pharisees. More importantly, both opinions expressed in these controversies in the Gospels are legitimately Jewish opinions in their context and time period, and their disagreement does not mean that Yeshua rejected all the teachings of the Pharisees and scribes. Instead, we are witnessing internal Jewish disputes recorded for us by the Gospel writers.

"And He answered them, saying, 'Why do you violate the commandment of God for the sake of your tradition? For God said, "Honor your father and mother," and "Anyone who curses his father and mother must be put to death." But you say that if a man says to his father or mother, "The help you might have received from me is a gift devoted to God," he is not to honor his father with it, so you then break the Word of God with your tradition.'"[1]

These words may need a little explanation. One thing necessary to understand this passage was the development of a rabbinic custom in those days by which it was possible to avoid giving charity and to help prevent robbery by declaring one's property to be dedicated to be a sacrifice for the Temple. Since thieves (at least Jewish ones) would be less likely to steal property belonging to God and the poor would have to do

---

1   Matthew 15:3-6

without rather than take God's goods, this custom temporarily saved one's property from others who wanted or needed it. Naturally, there was a way to undo this vow later in order to take back one's property for oneself.

Yeshua criticized this selfish attitude and practice, which allowed people to be greedy and withhold charity even from their needy parents by piously claiming they had already dedicated their possessions to God. The Ten Commandments say to honor (כבד) one's father and mother, which today people often interpret to mean a more conceptual idea of value and respect. This is not necessarily the intent of the word in biblical language, however. Abraham was *"honored/ respected/ loaded (כבד) with a great deal of possessions,"*[1] meaning that he owned a lot of (movable) property. It is because of this that the sons of Laban say, *"Jacob took everything our father had, and it is because of our father that he got all this honor/ property* (כבד)."[2] The word *honor* also means property in this passage. What can be interpreted from these comparisons means that honoring one's parents has something to do with property, that is to say that children should take care of their elderly and needy parents with material possessions. In more recent times, this principle has been turned on its head, and the State has to care for the elderly through Social Security (or in Israel through National Insurance pensions), instead of the elderly being financed by their own families. In fact, the Torah commands the opposite idea that the children take care of their aging parents who are no longer able to work. This is one of a very few commandments that comes with a promise: *"so that you may live long in the land which the Lord your*

---

1   Genesis 13:2

2   Genesis 31:1

God is giving you."[1] Too often people decide that God needs their money more than their parents do, without realizing that supporting one's parents is also giving to God, since He commanded it. Too many of us would rather contribute money to our synagogue or church and enjoy the honor and gratitude we receive from those institutions for our generosity, the tax deductions, and the feeling that we are contributing to "a higher cause." When we do this and neglect our needy parents, however, we are despising God's commandment to care for them.

This kind of behavior, which unfortunately the sages of Yeshua's day allowed, is condemned in Isaiah 29:13, *"And the Lord said, 'Because this people draw near with their mouth and honor me with their lips, while their hearts are far from me, and their fear of me is a commandment taught by men...'"* It is not unreasonable that Yeshua expounded upon this verse about false piety when He contrasted it with honoring one's father and mother in Matthew 15:8-9. This piety is false because the machinations of man uprooted it and turned it into something heartless and insincere. True worship of God does not consist of ceremonies or praise music, but rather in the keeping of his commandments. This is what James 1:27 means, *"Religion that is pure and undefiled before God the Father is this: to visit orphans and widows in their affliction and to keep oneself unstained from the world."* Yeshua's and Isaiah's words of criticism attack hypocritical human behavior in every place and time, within any kind of religious context. No religious group can give us immunity from our tendency to stray into this twisted deviation from the truth, and these words are not particularly meant to attack Jews in general or even Pharisees in particular, but rather all of us who prefer to

---

1 Exodus 20:12

honor God in ways that give us honor before men, instead of being faithful to the less conspicuous commandments.

In the same spirit Yeshua also added these words to his remarks in this situation, *"Hear and understand: it is not what goes into the mouth that defiles a person but what comes out of the mouth that defiles a person."*[1] Many people interpret this statement as a contradiction or a cancellation of the kosher laws in the Torah. Considering the context, it seems very clear that this was not the original intent of Yeshua's words. They are an intentionally exaggerated comparison, just like the words of the Prophets that seem to say that God does not desire sacrifices but rather acts of mercy, when He, in fact, commanded those very sacrifices along with mercy in the Torah.

The Torah actually says that a person who eats unclean food that is forbidden to him according to the dietary laws is rendered impure for a very short time, up to the same evening or the next day. Words, on the other hand, are impossible to cancel or take back once they leave our mouths and can do much more serious and far-reaching damage to ourselves and others. When Miriam spoke evil words against her brother Moses, God struck her from heaven with leprosy, a disease that makes the sufferer impure for a minimum of 21 days, far longer than what would have happened if she had eaten pork or shrimp. It is possible that Yeshua was even making a word play in Hebrew here between the words *metzora* (leprosy) and *motzi ra* (speaking evil). The Talmud forbids speaking evil about one's neighbor and even says that "anyone who embarrasses his fellow in public has shed his blood" (in other words, has murdered him). This is similar to Yeshua's words in Matthew 5:21-22 that say that anyone who speaks angry words of insult against his brother is the same as a murderer.

1   Matthew 15:11

When one compares these commandments, it seems as clear as daylight which one is more serious, though neither of them should cancel out the other.

When Yeshua's disciples asked Him about these words, they said, *"'Do you know that the Pharisees were offended [stumbled] when they heard this saying?' He answered, 'Every plant that my heavenly Father has not planted will be rooted up. Let them alone; they are blind guides. And if the blind leads the blind, both will fall into a pit.'"[1]* Even in these words there is a buried condemnation of the Pharisees for breaking this commandment from the Torah: *"Do not put a stumbling block before the blind."[2]* They stumbled over the words of Yeshua and were causing others to stumble even more by their blindness to the true spirit of the Torah, *"whose ways are ways of pleasantness, and all its paths are peace."[3]*

The main point and intention of Yeshua's words here is to distinguish between commandments given directly from God and the commandments of man. Some of the commandments of man may be perfectly legitimate and reasonable, but they do not hold the same weight and authority as the commandments of God and will not last forever. Traditions are not a negative thing; they are, in fact, the cultural codes by which humans live as societies under the direction of God. Tradition is our spiritual and cultural identity card that we cannot live without. Unfortunately, tradition that is merely *"a commandment taught by men"* and that does not consistently and consciously test its connection with the Word of God can distance us from the pure source of our faith, interfere with the connection between man and God, and most of all, distance people from one another by

1   Matthew 15:12-14

2   Leviticus 19:14

3   Proverbs 3:17

causing enmity and separation between them. The Prophets often talked about God's anger over the fact that his people had not united to serve Him in one accord. It is all too true that both the Church and the Jewish people have frequently sinned and continue to sin in this area.

One of the most prominent images Christians associate with the Pharisees comes from Yeshua's statement in Matthew 16:6, *"Beware of the leaven of the Pharisees and Sadducees."* The phrase the *leaven of the Pharisees* has come to symbolize the Jews and their "doctrine of lies that opposes the Law of the Messiah" in Church thought. This mistake stems from the fact that Matthew 16:12 explicitly identifies this phrase with *"the teaching of the Pharisees and Sadducees."* Yet the very combination of the Pharisees and Sadducees in this phrase should make us proceed cautiously when we remember that they were nearly complete opposites from one another in doctrine, theology, and *halacha*. The New Testament very infrequently combines them, condemning them together only for their hypocrisy and their lack of faith in Yeshua. Obviously, then, the "leaven" is not the Oral Law, belief in the resurrection, belief in angels and divine intervention, or any other of these important concepts upon which the Pharisees and Sadducees disagreed. The "leaven," or the problem of their teachings, must have been their testing of and lack of belief in Yeshua. In the immediate context before this verse of warning, the passage says that the Pharisees and Sadducees had come together to test Yeshua by demanding a miracle from Him. Knowing that they were just baiting Him, He refused to perform signs and wonders for them at that time. Miracles are never meant to inspire faith, and any faith that comes from them survives only until the next crisis comes along. Instead, miracles can only strengthen an already existing faith, and faith in Yeshua was something that both the Pharisees and Sadducees refused to even consider.

Having gone through these matters quickly, we will now turn to a long and important passage about the Pharisees to try to understand its point. It is paralleled in Luke 11, but we will examine Matthew's version since it is more infamous. Matthew 23:2-12 says, *"The scribes and the Pharisees sit on the seat of Moses, so practice and observe whatever they tell you–but not what they do. For they preach, but do not practice. They tie up heavy burdens, hard to bear, and lay them on people's shoulders, but they themselves are not willing to move them with their finger. They do all their deeds to be seen by others. For they make their tefillin (phylacteries) broad and their tzitzit (fringes) long, and they love the place of honor at feasts and the best seats in the synagogues and greetings in the marketplaces and being called rabbi by others. But you are not to be called rabbi, for you have one teacher, and you are all brothers. And call no man your father on earth, for you have one Father who is in heaven. Neither be called instructors, for you have one instructor, the Messiah. The greatest among you shall be your servant. Whoever exalts himself will be humbled, and whoever humbles himself will be exalted."*

At the very beginning of his words here, Yeshua establishes the authority of the scribes and the Pharisees to interpret the Torah and to make binding rulings on the Jewish public and on his disciples. One thing that confuses people about this passage is the fact that He says the scribes and the Pharisees *sit in the seat of Moses.* In the time of the Second Temple, this was the accepted expression for the seat of the preacher, the teacher, or the rabbi who publicly expounded on the Torah reading in the synagogue, interpreted the Torah, and guided the congregation in the way they should live their lives. His use of the expression *the seat of Moses* also shows Yeshua's agreement with the point of view later expounded in the Mishnah, in Pirkei Avot, which says that the chain of spiritual authority that began at Mount Sinai with Moses was passed down from generation to generation, even through the sages of Yeshua's day. It is true that after He established their authority in this passage, He went on to condemn them for their pursuit of glory and power, and especially their hypocrisy in failing to keep the commandments that they themselves established as binding on everyone else. Yeshua essentially said that they "talk the talk but do not walk the walk," as the expression goes, and He condemned this hypocrisy in them.

Since the charge of hypocrisy returns several times in Yeshua's words about the Pharisees and since many Christians mistakenly equate the word *Pharisees* with Jews in general and hypocrisy as a Jewish genetic trait passed down from generation to generation, let us examine this idea a little further. The word *hypocrite* comes from the Greek word *hypocrites*, which is defined as "a theater actor," in other words, a person who pretends to be someone other than himself. Many Christians began to equate hypocrites with Jews because of their misunderstanding of the New Testament and the linguistic source of this word. Unfortunately, this completely wrong understanding of Jews and Judaism has fueled the fires of anti-Semitism for many generations.

Yeshua was not saying that every Pharisee was a hypocrite but rather was condemning those among the Pharisees who were behaving like hypocrites because of their unethical behavior. Hypocrisy was not unique to Yeshua's day and age, of course, and we can all think of hypocrites in every religious context of our own time. The news media loves to expose religious hypocrites and smudge God's name in this way. Christianity has also had its share of hypocrites and every other kind of sin and wrongdoing that afflicts humanity as a whole. Yeshua's words here mimic the famous saying of the Hasmonean King Alexander Yannai to his wife Alexandra, "Do not be afraid either of the Pharisees or the Sadducees, but rather of the hypocrites who seem like Pharisees; they do the deeds of Zimri but expect the reward of Phineas."[1] (See Numbers 25 for the story of how the Israelite man Zimri worshipped idols and committed fornication with a Midianite woman as part of a great rebellion that aroused God's wrath against Israel. It was only the zeal of Phineas in killing Zimri and the woman involved in the act of adultery that turned away God's wrath and stopped the judgment. For this act Phineas received the right of the priesthood as his reward).

We must differentiate between Yeshua's criticisms of the Sadducees, who ran the Temple service but who were considered corrupt, and the Pharisees, whom the common people believed to be faithful to the Torah. The people placed the Pharisees under a magnifying glass to examine their behavior and imitate it. This is why Yeshua said, *"If your righteousness does not exceed that of the scribes and the Pharisees, you will not enter the kingdom of heaven."*[2] What does this mean, and what is the righteousness Yeshua ascribes to them when He says ours has to exceed it? Their "righteousness" means the accepted standard of that society for a life of faith and ethics demanded by the command of God. In this respect the Pharisees and scribes represent the accepted positive norms of behavior, but Yeshua was preaching a special kind of *Hasidism* (piety), which goes above and beyond the expected norms in

1   bSotah 22

2   Matthew 5:20

the quest to please God. In order to truly know God, one has to rise to a higher level than the accepted norms and rules of the Pharisees, (which, incidentally, were much higher than the accepted ethical norms of our society today).

When Yeshua criticized the Pharisees, it was for their lack of faith or their straying from the straight path of honesty and righteousness. This kind of accusation is internally driven from someone who is already inside the camp and wants to fix it, rather than an outside enemy who means to destroy. Correcting the mistakes of our neighbors in love is a commandment from both the Torah and the New Testament, as Leviticus 19:17 says, *"You shall not hate your brother in your heart, but you shall surely reason with him so that you will not bear sin on his account."* Similarly, Galatians 6:1 says, *"Brothers, if anyone is caught in any transgression, you who are spiritual should restore him gently. But watch yourselves, lest you also be tempted."* In other words, correcting our brothers and sisters in love, gentleness, and humility is important so that we will not be responsible for their sin through our silence. This is what Yeshua did among his generation, and this is always the correct thing to do.

The Prophets are full of this kind of "constructive criticism" that speaks very harshly against the political and spiritual leaders of the people who had fallen away from the ways of the Lord. The majority of Prophets received only hatred and enmity from the people and the leaders, who often persecuted, jailed, and killed them for their words of correction. Eventually, however, these same Prophets became holy martyrs in our eyes, and we know that they sought only goodness for our people. Similarly, Yeshua protested the distorted ways and faulty ethics of the leaders of his days that were ripping apart the fabric of society and bringing about its humiliating subjugation by harsh foreign powers. This bad leadership contributed to the destruction of the Jewish people, the abandonment of good character, the split of the people into various disputing sects, baseless hatred, and civil wars. Even the sages attributed the destruction of the Temple to baseless hatred. Yet Yeshua was full of love for Israel and faith in the eternal significance and role of Israel, which unfortunately many of his present-day followers are unable to see.

When we hear criticism coming from within the system, we know it has greater weight and significance than external criticism, which does not understand the rules, goals, and procedures of that system. When the opposition party says something negative about the government, we only half listen to them because we expect them to oppose the government; that is their job as the opposition. We might even expect them to say things that are exaggerated and only half true, just to make a point. However, when someone belonging to the party in power openly criticizes the government or the way things are being run, we sit up and take notice because we recognize that he knows what he is talking about. The one who corrects from within is a partner on the road to the same goals who simply knows that there are inconsistencies between the stated goals and the actions that really occur. Unless a person identifies closely with the group he critiques, he would simply leave that group and find someone else who more closely shares his values.

The religious structure in Israel at the time of Yeshua was very similar to what it is today in the modern state of Israel. Today we have the Chief Rabbinate, which is supposed to be the highest religious authority but which is commonly perceived as a corrupt and antiquated institution infected with politics, immorality, and spiritual weakness. There are many groups of

Torah-observant Jews in Israel who refuse to even recognize this institution or its authority over them, and their criticism is much more noteworthy and to the point than the negative words of the secular Jews who condemn it from the outside. This is exactly how we should understand the relationship between Yeshua and the rest of the Jewish world during his life on earth. When He protested against the Pharisees, He had important points to make and was not completely disparaging their world-view or their faith; instead, He condemned their unethical behavior. Yeshua stood closer to the world-view of the Pharisees than any other religious group of his day because He, like them, believed in angels, eternal life, free will, the revelation at Sinai, the words of the Prophets, the Oral Law, and the entire spiritual structure of faith that was built on the same foundation as the one the Pharisees had.

The New Testament refers to Yeshua many times as "teacher" or "rabbi" and to his followers as "disciples" or "students," terms which disappear altogether after Acts 21:16. These terms were very common in the Pharisaic context from which they originated, so one might well ask why they stopped being used in the early Church. Perhaps one explanation is that after Yeshua returned to heaven, different aspects of his character and mission came to the forefront as the focus shifted to carrying the Gospel to the nations. The memory of Yeshua as a teacher of the Torah and as a local rabbi dimmed as his disciples spread throughout the world. The men who had known Him personally as their rabbi and teacher were responsible for the writing of the Gospels and their picture of Yeshua, but the next generation of his followers who had never met Him in the flesh began to emphasize other aspects of his mission. Too many of us in this generation have also forgotten that Yeshua was a great rabbi whose teaching about the Torah was a light that explained and illuminated the Word of God far better than any other rabbi who has ever lived. In addition to his other roles, Yeshua will always be a great teacher and rabbi, as long as there exist disciples of his who will study his words as eternal truth from God.

Let us now continue by examining this important text that involves Yeshua's relationship with the Pharisees in Matthew 23. Since the text is very long, we will discuss it piece by piece in an attempt to understand it correctly. Verses 13-15 say, *"But woe to you, scribes and Pharisees, hypocrites. For you shut the kingdom of heaven in people's faces. For you neither enter yourselves, nor allow those who would enter to go in. Woe to you, scribes and Pharisees, hypocrites. For you travel across sea and land to make a single proselyte, and when he becomes a proselyte, you make him twice as much a child of hell as yourselves."* These are very strong charges which first demand that we have a basic understanding of Yeshua's use of the phrase "kingdom of heaven," since He accuses the scribes and Pharisees of preventing people from entering it.

Traditional Christian interpretation tends to say that the kingdom of heaven is the world to come, or the life after death promised to the righteous in the Garden of Eden. This interpretation turns the kingdom of heaven into some kind of abstract reality that has nothing to do with this world and which completely excludes any participation by the scribes or Pharisees. This understanding is incorrect, however, so we must try to uncover the meaning of the phrase "kingdom of heaven" (or "kingdom of God") as it was used in Yeshua's time. This kingdom is not hidden in heaven, but rather is present here on earth among humanity. Yeshua Himself proclaimed its coming with these words in Matthew 3:17, *"Repent, for the kingdom of heaven is near."* These words are the fulfillment of the prophecy in Isaiah 52:7, *"How beautiful on the mountains are the feet of him who brings good news, who announces peace, tells news of goodness, announces salvation, and says to Zion, 'Your God reigns.'"*

To "enter into the kingdom of heaven" means to know God and the effects that knowledge causes on our present and future lives in the world. Yeshua is ruling this world even now when we cannot always see it, and as citizens of the kingdom of God, we are supposed to help build the kingdom and bring it completely into submission to the rule of the one true God through our actions. Naturally, there is a lot more to the kingdom of Heaven than our current lives, but what we do during our lifetimes for the kingdom of God matters immensely both for the present and future kingdom. Our good deeds are building for the kingdom and will eventually be important parts of God's new creation. We are not merely "waiting out our time" on this earth until we escape to God's kingdom "in the sky by-and-by," but rather are living in and helping establish the beginning phases of the kingdom of God on earth.

One scholar beautifully summarizes these principles this way, "Faced with his beautiful and powerful creation in rebellion, God longed to set it right, to rescue it from continuing corruption and impending chaos and to bring it back into order and fruitfulness. God longed, in other words, to re-establish his wise sovereignty over the whole creation, which would mean a great act of healing and rescue. He did not want to rescue humans *from* creation any more than He wanted to rescue Israel *from* the Gentiles. He wanted to rescue Israel *in order that Israel might be a light to the Gentiles,* and He wanted thereby to rescue humans *in order that humans might be his rescuing stewards over creation.* That is the inner dynamic of the kingdom of God. That, in other words, is how the God who made humans to be his stewards over creation and who called Israel to be the light of the world is to become king, in accordance with his original intention in creation, on the one hand, and his original intention in the covenant, on the other. To snatch saved souls away to a disembodied heaven would destroy the whole point. God is to become king of the whole world at last. And He will do this not by declaring that the inner dynamic of creation (that it be ruled by humans) was a mistake, nor by declaring that the inner dynamic of his covenant (that Israel would be the means of saving the nations) was a failure, but rather by fulfilling them both."[1]

Now that the meaning of the kingdom of Heaven is clear, we must ask, "What do these accusations that the Pharisees were keeping the flock of Israel from entering the kingdom of heaven mean?" One of the ways that people get to know God is through their spiritual leaders and parents, both in Christianity and Judaism. In this sense, we are like children. Children's understanding of God's nature is greatly connected with their relationship with their parents and how their parents behave toward them. Our parents, as well as our pastors, rabbis, and other spiritual leaders, serve as examples to us of how God cares about us, what his nature is, and what He expects from us. When parents or spiritual leaders fail and fall into the hypocrisy of saying one thing and doing another, they are demonstrating to their children (whether spiritual or physical) that God also behaves that way.

When a child is very young, he can bear a lot of hypocrisy from his parents because he assumes that whatever they do must be perfect; but when he reaches the stage of adolescence, he begins to see that his parents are not nearly as perfect as the

1   Wright, N.T. *Surprised by Hope*. New York: HarperOne, 2008, p. 202.

façade they portray to the outside world. This is one reason why the teenage years are so difficult, since the once "perfect" authority figures become subject to critical observations of how inconsistent they really are. The same thing happens to many people when they reach "spiritual adolescence" and begin to critically observe the religious world around them, which is, unfortunately, full of examples of religious leaders who do not practice what they preach. All too often these bad shepherds cause many of their sheep to fall away from the faith through their disappointment in their leaders.

The non-religious public also looks to famous religious leaders as examples of what religion and God are all about, so every time a new religious scandal hits the news, it is another blow to God's reputation in the world and a desecration of his name. Maybe this is a good time to remember that each one of us who claims to be a child of God bears his name everywhere we go in this world and therefore has a responsibility to behave in a way that brings Him glory instead of a bad reputation. When we engage in corruption and sin, we drive people farther away from the knowledge of the truth and from a relationship with God because they assume that He must be just like his followers. This terrible reality is exactly what Yeshua refers to in this passage that condemns the Pharisees and the scribes. They may teach the right way to approach God, but they themselves refuse to do it when they continue to sin, therefore shutting the common people out from the true knowledge of God. Their hypocrisy, not their teaching, is distancing those who would seek God from the door to a relationship with Him. Yeshua says that these men go to great lengths to spread their teaching, even going so far as to travel across the world as missionaries to make converts, but end up only driving people farther away from God because of their corrupt behavior.

This last charge sounds very strange to Jews today, since it has been a long time since Judaism actually tried to convert non-Jews on a large scale. Yet in the time of Yeshua and even until the Fourth Century, converting to Judaism, or at least becoming a "God-fearer" who kept some of the commandments of the Torah, was actually a very popular thing, especially in the upper class Roman society. First Century Judaism was definitely a missionary religion, which is why Paul's journeys all over the world to share the Gospel were considered in character for Jews of his time. Eventually, conversion to Judaism became so popular that the Roman Empire completely forbade it and imposed severe penalties on any Jew who encouraged it or helped a non-Jew become Jewish. Out of their fear of these punishments, the rabbis banned converting non-Jews for some time and decreed that any potential convert had to be discouraged from becoming a Jew. This is why most forms of Judaism today still discourage conversion and make it very difficult for anyone who persists in a desire to become Jewish if he or she was not born that way.

The truth is, however, that God called the Jews to be a light to the nations and to spread the knowledge of Him to every corner of the world. The Jews are responsible to be the "priests" of the world and to mediate between God and the nations, something which far more Jews realized back in Yeshua's time. Some Jewish writers from the period even viewed the exile as God's ideal program to educate the non-Jewish world about the God of Israel, instead of seeing it merely as a punishment for sin. They therefore made great efforts to make converts, and some people even say that the great sage Rabbi Akiva was a convert to Judaism. It is also highly likely that Luke, the author of the Gospel of Luke and Acts as well as the companion of Paul on his missionary journeys, was a convert or a "God-fearer" who was not born a Jew but who sought to know the one true God through Judaism.

Although Paul's letters often speak about the matter of Gentile converts to Judaism, Yeshua really never mentions that phenomenon at all, except for this passage. Therefore one should try to understand what He means here by saying that they become "sons of hell." There are several possible meanings to this condemnation, not the least of which is that people who convert to any religion can become so fanatical about their new religion that they begin to hate and despise everyone who does not have their same zeal and level of religiosity, to the point that their company becomes unbearable. Zeal for God is a wonderful thing, but zeal has to be seasoned with grace, love, and humility if we expect our passion for God to be attractive to anyone else. If we pridefully try to be "more Catholic than the Pope" (or "more Jewish than the Chief Rabbi") and despise everyone who does not match up to our standards, then we are breaking more important biblical principles about loving our neighbors. Arrogance makes our presence as unbearable as hell would be to the people around us, and it characterizes the sons of darkness rather than the sons of light. Most converts naturally follow the behaviors and beliefs of their spiritual fathers, so any converts of these corrupt Pharisees about whom Yeshua speaks here were likely to be truly awful people, unless they followed Yeshua's advice to his disciples to, "Do what they say but not what they do."

Yeshua's complaints about this group of Pharisees are further illustrated in the next few verses of this passage. *"Woe to you, blind guides, who say, 'If anyone swears by the Temple it is nothing[1], but if anyone swears by the gold of the Temple, he is bound by his oath.' You blind fools! For which is greater,*

---

1   The Greek translation here misses the Hebrew meaning of *not convicted.*

the gold or the Temple that has made the gold sacred? And you say, 'If anyone swears by the altar, it is nothing, but if anyone swears by the gift that is on the altar, he is bound by his oath.' You blind man! For which is greater, the gift or the altar that makes the gift sacred? So whoever swears by the altar swears by it and everything on it. And whoever swears by the Temple swears by it and by him who dwells in it. And whoever swears by heaven swears by the throne of God and by him who sits upon it."[1]

The matter of the exact wording of oaths and contracts was a big point of dispute among the rabbis and sages for many centuries before Yeshua's time and long afterwards as well. The Talmud is full of passages discussing the exact wording a contract or oath must have to be valid in a court of law. While the sages understood the importance and power of words, they got so caught up in the details of which words would include all the possible exceptions and considerations that it became easy to lose track of the important biblical principal of being people of truth and honesty in everything one says and does. Oaths were a matter of great dispute and importance in Yeshua's society because the man who swore an oath properly could be released from it only with great difficulty. Some teachers such as Yeshua exposed the problem with this kind of focus on the details of oaths without attention to the principles of truth and justice and advised their disciples to refrain from swearing oaths at all. This passage is an example of his stance on this question, and we also see his position strongly in Matthew 5:33-37, *"Again you have heard that it was said to those of old, 'You shall not swear falsely but shall perform to the Lord what you have sworn.' But I say to you: do not take an oath at all, either by heaven, for it is the throne of God, or by the*

1   Matthew 23:16-22

earth, for it is his footstool, or by Jerusalem for it is the city of the great King. And do not take an oath by your head, for you cannot make one hair white or black. Let what you say be simply 'yes' or 'no;' anything more than this comes from evil."

In today's society hardly anyone takes an oath on something (other than perhaps a Bible in the occasional American courtroom, a practice which is becoming more rare), so it is easy to misunderstand the significance of swearing on something holy in ancient times. Someone who says, "I swear by my head to pay Person A such-and-such an amount of money," would essentially be saying that if he did not keep his word, then he was invoking a curse on his head and giving God permission to kill him. Likewise, a person who takes an oath on a Bible, the Temple, heaven, the throne of God, Jerusalem, God, or any holy object is really saying that if he breaks his word (even inadvertently), he invites all the curses that would come from defiling the holiness of one of those things to come upon him. What Yeshua teaches here is that we should be people of our word without having to invoke such curses on ourselves when we promise something. Only conditions out of our control should keep us from fulfilling a promise, just as we cannot control whether our hair is (naturally) white or black. Our reputation for honesty should be so great that people immediately believe us when we say we will or will not do something, even without invoking curses or heavenly punishments upon ourselves.

As for understanding the words about blind guides, let us look first to Deuteronomy 27:18, which says, *"Cursed be anyone who misleads a blind man on the road."* Isaiah 3:12 mourns for Israel with these words, *"O my people, your guides mislead you, and they have swallowed up the course of your paths.*" Spiritual and political leaders are supposed to lead their people on the right path, especially back in the times when the ability to read was uncommon. A person who cannot read the Word of God for himself is essentially blind without the aid of a guide. One who guides a physically or spiritually blind person has a responsibility to lead the blind man accurately, something which can only be done if the guide himself can see correctly.

This is a point Yeshua emphasizes in this parable in Luke 6:39-42. *"He also told them a parable. 'Can a blind man lead a blind man? Will they not both fall into a pit? A disciple is not above his teacher, but everyone when he is fully trained will be like his teacher. Why do you see the speck that is in your brother's eye, but do not notice the log that is in your own eye? How can you say to your brother, "Brother, let me take out the speck that is in your eye," when you yourself do not see the log that is in your own eye? You hypocrite, first take the log out of your own eye, and then you will see clearly to take out the speck that is in your brother's eye.'"* By calling these Pharisees "blind guides" in Matthew 23, Yeshua says that they are cursed for leading others astray and will only end up falling into the pit of hell together as they ignore their own sins in order to condemn the sins of others. This is the definition of hypocrisy, which unfortunately was not restricted to some Pharisees of Yeshua's day, but rather continues to plague the ranks of religions of all varieties unto this day. Spiritual guides have a great responsibility to understand what and where the destination is so that they can bring both themselves and their followers safely to the goal by the right road.

Yeshua's strong words continue in Matthew 23:23-24, *"Woe to you, scribes and Pharisees, hypocrites. For you tithe mint, dill, and cumin and have neglected the weightier matters of the law: justice and mercy and faithfulness. These you ought to have done without neglecting the others. You blind guides, straining out a gnat and swallowing a camel."* Before getting down to the point of these statements, let us quickly remember that according to the Torah, it is obligatory to tithe every crop grown in the land of Israel to God and the priests. It is also important to know that the Torah forbids consuming gnats (and most kinds of bugs), as well as unclean mammals such as camels. With this in mind, let us return to the main point here, which is that great stringency in "little commandments," such as tithing herbs grown in Israel or checking one's vegetables to make sure that one does not accidentally consume bugs, must not distract our attention away from more important commandments, such as justice, mercy, and faithfulness.

Yeshua does not cancel the validity of these smaller commandments and in fact even upholds them. Yet He says that there is little value in keeping them if we allow ourselves to violate the great ethical obligations of the Torah and the duties of the heart. The Prophets of Israel said the same things when they said that God desired mercy and not sacrifice. Many liberal Bible scholars like to think that the Prophets were an anti-Temple group of Israelites, but they misunderstand the typical Ancient Near Eastern language of exaggeration and relative importance. The Prophets did not forbid sacrifices, as they were obedient to the Torah that commanded them in the first place. Rather, they taught that without ethical behavior, all the ceremonies and sacrifices in the world would not help anyone gain favor in God's eyes. The very idea of being careful not to eat unkosher gnats but in so doing swallowing an entire unkosher camel is meant to be exaggerated and ridiculous sounding to make this point visibly memorable to the audience. As a teacher who stood firmly within Jewish tradition and in the words of the Torah, Yeshua could easily relate to the debates of *halacha* of his day, adding points, quibbling over details when necessary, but most of all, reminding his followers of the larger principles on which we must base our lives and our observance of the commandments at all times if our good deeds are to be for the sake of heaven and not merely for our own ego or glory.

The passage continues with these words, *"Woe to you, scribes and Pharisees, hypocrites! For you clean the outside of the cup and the plate, but inside they are full of greed and self-indulgence. You blind Pharisees! First clean the inside of the cup and plate, that the outside may also be clean. Woe to you, scribes and Pharisees, hypocrites! For you are like whitewashed tombs, which appear outwardly beautiful, but within are full of dead people's bones and all uncleanness. So you also outwardly appear righteous to others, but within you are full of hypocrisy and lawlessness."*[1] These words also contain many clues and "insider *halachic* language" relating to internal Jewish disputes of Yeshua's day and are therefore far more than an argument about how to wash dishes or descriptions of tombs. It is clear that a description of a dish that is clean on the outside and dirty on the inside is a perfect metaphor for a hypocrite of any religion, but there is more to this passage than that.

The key to understanding the more nuanced elements in these words lies in the importance of purity and impurity in the discourse and lives of Second Temple Period Jews. A quick glance through the Torah reveals a huge quantity of laws dealing with how a person or object could become ritually "clean" or "unclean" from childbirth, death, sickness, food, or just regular daily occurrences. One's state of purity or impurity

1   Matthew 23:25-28

mattered a great deal if that person wanted to approach God in the Tabernacle (or later the Temple) because it was forbidden to enter these sacred spaces in a state of impurity. The Torah orders that if an unclean animal carcass fell into certain kinds of dishes, the dish became permanently impure and had to be destroyed. By the time of the Second Temple Period, the sages had enacted many more purity laws about dishes of various kinds of materials, depending on how absorbent they were, and how to purify them either by putting them in fire for a set amount of time or immersing them in a *mikveh* (ritual bath). Stone, for example, was considered to be the most difficult kind of dish to pollute and so became the material of choice for dishes in various Jewish cities of the time period, especially Jerusalem.

Arguments about these issues were still alive and controversial in Yeshua's day, and therefore the Pharisees would have keyed in immediately to the terminology of his discourse here. It would obviously be foolish to ritually purify the outside of a dish to make it sparkling clean and yet leave the inside full of disgusting and unhealthy bacteria or sources of impurity that would keep polluting it from the inside out. Similarly, religious hypocrites do their best to present a polished and perfect appearance to everyone around them while secretly harboring serious sins like greed and selfishness that no one can see except for God, the One whose opinion matters the most. Religious hypocrites live for the approval of man while ignoring the dark sins of their inmost beings, something of which all religious people need to be careful. Yeshua says we must cleanse ourselves of our inmost sins just as much as we should worry about our outward appearance of righteousness.

The next metaphor Yeshua uses here to describe hypocrites is that of a hidden tomb. Dead bodies were one of the main sources of ritual impurity, and the details of *"tumat hamet"* (impurity of death) were extremely important issues in the discussions of the sages about the *halachot* of purity. For example, if a person died inside a house, that entire house became unclean for seven days, and a grave was a permanent source of impurity. Anyone who came into contact with a grave became ritually impure for seven days as well, and priests were forbidden to approach graves or graveyards at all, lest they become too impure to serve in the Temple service. In Yeshua's generation the entire city of Tiberias was forbidden to priests and ritually observant Jews because it had been built on top of an ancient graveyard. Today in Israel, graveyards are carefully marked with big signs warning people of priestly descent to take the long way around them and not to get so close that they become impure. Obviously then, a tomb that had been whitewashed and hidden was a serious matter because it had the potential to lead unwary passers-by into sin without even knowing it.

Hypocrisy is like this, too; the hypocrite deceives those around him into thinking that he is a model of holiness, while he leads them deeper into sin. This charge is not unique to Jews, and it is wrong to assume that Yeshua's words only applied to Pharisees. We, too, as religious people, must be careful about our inner as well as our outer state of purity and holiness. Please note that Yeshua's last sentence here says that his listeners were full of hypocrisy and lawlessness. He was not rebuking them for their verbal concern for the details of the Torah, for, in fact, that is important, but rather for their lack of physically keeping the very Torah that they upheld only with their words instead of also with their actions.

The point here ought to be very clear. Yeshua says nothing against the rules of purity for dishes, but rather includes them in a larger framework of principles that the Torah obligates. If a person refuses to share his food with the needy, it does not matter how careful he is to keep his dishes and his food kosher; God will not be pleased with his selfishness. One good reason to keep one's food and dishes pure and kosher, especially in Israel, is so that one will be able to share with the needy around him, many of whom are able to eat only in kosher establishments. If we refuse to share with the needy, then all of our other actions become impure because of our egocentric lack of concern for others. The same principle applies with our church and synagogue buildings. We love to build enormous, beautiful buildings filled with the most intricate decorations and furnishings and the latest technology. Yet if the hearts and actions of the leaders and worshippers are not pure, humble, and righteous before God, our songs, prayers, offerings, Torah readings, and sermons will mean nothing to Him.

The rest of this passage in Matthew 23 applies mostly to the Pharisaic leaders of Yeshua's generation and the coming destruction of the Temple by the Romans. What is most important to realize when reading strongly critical passages like these in which Yeshua condemns the religious leaders of his day is that these charges can just as easily be laid against ourselves and our own religious institutions today and therefore cannot be used as ammunition for anti-Semitism, anti-Rabbinism, or antinomianism. These words are found in the New Testament because they contain important principles and warnings for every believer and are not just there to condemn the Pharisees and the scribes. If that was all these passages meant, there would be no need for them to be in the New Testament today. Instead, these truths should convict all of us to our very core to examine our hearts, motivations, and actions to make sure we are not leading others astray or rejecting the true and acceptable worship of our God through hypocrisy.

Yeshua could say these difficult words to the Pharisees because they were his people, from his milieu and background, and He similarly calls his people today, both Jews and non-Jews, to judge and cleanse themselves in light of his words. It is impossible to be sure if Yeshua actually was a Pharisee Himself, but it is obvious that He lived very close to them in their world of discourse and deed. His words were meant to convict them and bring them to repentance, not to condemn them and the entire Jewish people for all time. The Church has misunderstood and misapplied these important words far too long, and we as believers of our own time must wake up and take them to heart so we can stop falling into the very trap Yeshua warned against so many years ago. Ecclesiastes says there is nothing new under the sun, and it is true that the character of humanity has not changed for the better in the last several thousand years. No Jew, Christian, or Messianic Jew is exempt from an inclination to hypocrisy, and this spiritual disease is just as strong in us as it was in the sages of the Second Temple Period. May we all merit to be enlightened guides who lead ourselves and others with the light of God's Word while we constantly test the truth and sincerity of our own hearts and lives.

Chapter Five:

Turn Your Face Toward Jerusalem

Luke 9:51 says, *"And it came about when the days were approaching for his ascension that he resolutely set his face to go to Jerusalem."* Another translation says, *"When the days were approaching for his ascension he was determined to go to Jerusalem."* This is a rather simple text without any difficult words that has both a simple literary meaning and an important spiritual or *"drash"* (exegetically expounded) meaning. In this chapter we intend to use this level of interpretation for this verse in order to apply it to a very important message for the Church of today.

First let us examine the beginning of the verse on this level. *"When the days were approaching"* is similar to the common New Testament phrase, *"when his hour had come."* There are several places in the New Testament that mention *"His hour had come"* or *"It is not my time yet"* or *"My time has come."* In John 7:6, the apostles in the Galilee during the Feast of Tabernacles tell Yeshua, *"Let us go to Jerusalem,"* but He tells them, *"My time has not come yet."* Luke 9 now informs us that his hour had finally come.

If I say, "The hour has come for me to leave the house and go to the congregation," it means that I have a calendar. I have an agenda, and when I look at my program, I know when my time has come and when my time has not come. God also has a calendar and an agenda, and He knows the appropriate times and the seasons far better than we do. Paul in Galatians 4:4 says, *"When the time had fully come, God sent his Son..."*

It was the right time, and it was something that was marked, in a manner of speaking, with red ink on God's calendar. Yeshua knew He had a calendar appointment in Jerusalem and that it was his time to go there. The word *resolutely* is very interesting in this verse. It means that He made up his mind to go to Jerusalem, no matter who would try to distract Him on the way, and at all costs. He had a calendar, and He knew when his appointment was due to come.

Why did Yeshua have to go to Jerusalem, and what did He have to do there that caused Him to turn his face toward it *resolutely*? Every Evangelical Protestant will tell you that He had to go to Jerusalem to die, but they are not paying attention to the text when they say this. We have almost 1,500 years of Christian history that, with all of its beauty and tradition, has mesmerized us and numbed us from seeing what God has for us in his Word. In Christianity people like to see Yeshua hanging on the cross, but they do not like Him to come and sit next to them in their congregation. The text speaks of his ascension, which is far more important than his death because it proved He was no mere messianic pretender, but rather, *the* Messiah of God.

I went to university in Nashville, Tennessee, for two years, and I did not have a car at that time. Therefore, on Saturdays I walked from where I lived to the Orthodox synagogue, and on Sundays I walked from where I lived to the church that was right across the street from the Orthodox synagogue. One Sunday in 1969, I got to church early, and I noticed that the rabbi was in his office with the light on in the synagogue. The church was still closed, so I went to talk to the rabbi for a little while. He knew that I was a Jew from Israel who believed in Yeshua, but he still invited me to have a cup of coffee with him in his office. While we were talking in his office, all of a sudden he got up, went to the window, looked out of it, and said, "Joe, do you see all these people going to church? I have been a rabbi here for thirteen years, and nobody from this church has ever knocked on my door or invited me to anything. Isn't it strange that they go in there every Sunday and worship a dead Jew hanging on a tree but don't like the live Jews?" This story is sad and sounds extreme in light of all today's ecumenical movements and Jewish-Christian dialogue meetings, but this attitude is probably more common than we want to admit.

That is how it is with Yeshua. Most Christianity stops at the cross, and ninety percent of all our attention is focused on Him hanging on the cross and his bleeding and suffering. This statement is not meant to diminish the seriousness of the cross of Yeshua or minimize his suffering. We cannot deny the atonement of our sins by the blood of Yeshua the Messiah. That is a central point of our faith and our relationship to the Almighty God of Israel. If we stop at the cross, however, we have no life. If there is no resurrection and ascension, and if Yeshua is not sitting at the right hand of God right now, then our faith is in vain. Too many Christians focus only on the cross and then perhaps once a year on Easter remember the resurrection, while almost entirely ignoring Yeshua's ascension to begin his rule of the kingdom of God.

Believing in Yeshua's ascension and not confusing it as being the same thing as his resurrection is extremely important if we are to properly understand his mission to the world and our future hope for his return to earth to make all things right. The Anglican scholar and theologian N.T. Wright has some interesting comments on the importance of the ascension and how it helps the believer to know that Yeshua is already in some way ruling the world from the right hand of the Father. "To embrace the ascension is to heave a sigh of relief, to give up the struggle to be God (and with it the inevitable despair at our constant failure), and to enjoy our status as *creatures:* image-bearing creatures, but creatures nonetheless. The ascension thus speaks of the Jesus who remains truly human and hence in an important sense absent from us while in another equally important sense present to us in a new way."[1]

This text in Luke 9 says that Yeshua went to Jerusalem for his ascension. He was homeward bound; the cross was only a necessary and important station along the way through which He had to go. That was not the goal or where He wanted to stay. He wanted to pass by the cross and ascend to heaven to be with the Father. If we, as disciples of Yeshua, do not move beyond the cross to think about going home, seeing Him descend from the clouds, and our present fellowship with Him, then we are more miserable than any other religious group in the world. That is the difference between the traditional Christian worldview and what the Bible says. Our faith is not in a crucified Messiah; it is a faith in a living Messiah who is coming back. In order for us to grasp the simplicity of this, we have to do what Yeshua did and set our faces one more time toward Jerusalem. Let the Church set its face toward Jerusalem and away from the traditions we have inherited from paganism and Rome! We are being robbed of the joy of life that comes through faith in Yeshua the Messiah. Just like Yeshua, who set his face toward Jerusalem, our attention and our focus needs to be on the parts of our faith that come from Jerusalem.

Many Christians think their religion is a serious and sad business instead of being bright and joyous in the Lord. They think that there is something wrong and frivolous about joyful believers. Yeshua's resurrection, however, should change our

1 Wright, N. T. *Surprised by Hope.* New York: HarperOne, 2008, p. 114.

sadness into joy. We believe in a living Messiah, not a Jew hanging on a tree, but one raised from the grave.

Too much of Christianity is connected to Rome by the umbilical cord, no matter whether they are Baptists, Methodists, Charismatics, Churches of Christ, Catholics, or anyone else. Most Protestant Church history books trace their roots to Luther in Germany, to Calvin in Switzerland, to Menno Simons in Holland, to the Anabaptists in Europe, or to the Pentecostals in Azuza Street. Rome became the center of the Catholic Church only by a series of political and religious accidents; there is no command in the Bible for such a thing.

That is not my Church or the Church for which Yeshua died. The Church for which Yeshua died is not a Gentile Church, and it looks toward Jerusalem, not Rome. Jerusalem was clearly the head of the Church in the book of Acts back when the Church was still primarily composed of Jews. People think that it is acceptable for Rome to be the head of the Church because the Church is "mainly Gentile now." The truth, however, is that there are no Gentiles in the Church. Each believer has been made a fellow citizen of the same city, which is not Paris, London, Dallas, or Rome. It is Jerusalem! Those who were formerly Gentiles have been grafted into the covenant of Abraham and have been transformed into part of the people of God, whose center should be in Israel, the chosen land and people of God.

The Restoration of Israel and the Restoration of the Church go hand in hand. Luke 9:51-56 says, *"As the time approached for him to be taken up to heaven, Yeshua resolutely set out for Jerusalem. And he sent messengers on ahead, who went into a Samaritan village to get things ready for him, but the people there did not welcome him because he was heading for Jerusalem. When the disciples Ya'akov and Yochanon saw this, they asked, 'Lord, do you want us to call fire down from heaven to destroy them?' But Yeshua turned and rebuked them, and they went to another village."* An alternate manuscript of the New Testament also adds here, *"Yeshua said to them, 'You do not know what kind of spirit you are of, for the Son of Man did not come to destroy lives, but to save them.'"*

In this story, Yeshua was going to Jerusalem in the springtime before Passover, and the Land of Israel is absolutely beautiful and green during this time. Most of the year, we do not have any rain. In March we occasionally still have a little rain, and it is warm enough for the wildflowers to sprout on the hills. Sometimes the hills are almost totally red with poppies, and the view of the land is absolutely spectacular. Yeshua and His disciples walked through the Galilee during this beautiful season to Jerusalem, and then they came to Samaria.

The Samaritans are a group of people comprised of a mix of people from the ten Northern tribes that Nebuchadnezzar had exiled and people that Nebuchadnezzar had sent to Samaria from other countries. The Jews hated the Samaritans; and because they suffered from prejudice, the Samaritans, in turn, became prejudiced against the Jews and against Jerusalem. They had their own spiritual capital on Mount Gerizim, which is still the religious center for the Samaritans today near Nablus in the West Bank. So when the disciples of Yeshua were looking for a place for Him to spend the night and came to this Samaritan village, the people of the village asked Him where He was going. When the disciples answered, "Jerusalem," the villagers said, "There is no room for you in this village." Their racial prejudice kept Yeshua out of their village. Just think how much they lost! Everywhere that Yeshua went, He healed people, raised people from the dead, fed the hungry, opened the eyes of the blind, and purified the lepers. Wherever Yeshua went, there were signs and wonders and miracles, but these people kept Him and his miracles out of their village because of their racial prejudice against Jerusalem.

Any time that there is racial prejudice, there is no room for Yeshua. Any time that people are anti-Semitic, there is no room for Yeshua either. The essence of faith in one God is that we have one Father, and if we have one Father, it means that we are all brothers. In any place of racial prejudice, there is no monotheism because prejudice is a denial of the fact that we are brothers and that we have one common fate. Those who are prejudiced deny that there is one Ruler, who created everything in the world, from the elephant to the ant.

It was wrong for these Samaritans to keep Yeshua out of their village because of their prejudice; but the disciples, the two brothers, the Sons of Thunder, Yaakov and Yochanan, were also wrong. These disciples spent three years with Yeshua and were even there at the Sermon on the Mount and when He fed the 5,000. They walked with Him, heard Him teach, and saw Him do miracles, but they were incensed that this Samaritan village prevented them from spending the night there. They got so angry over these people's prejudice that they asked Yeshua for permission to "Burn this village down! We know you have the power and that you are greater than Elijah!" Samaria was the land of Elijah, the place of his origin and his operation. Elijah called down fire several times and burned up the servants and soldiers of King Ahab, who came to arrest him. Three times he called fire down from heaven, and fifty soldiers were burned up in an instant, like *Star Wars* or some other action movie. The disciples thought that Yeshua ought to do the same in order to punish the inhospitable Samaritans in his day.

Yeshua knew better, though. He knew that the Church is not supposed to demonstrate the power of God in violence and vengeance; it is supposed to work out the power of God to win the world, seek for the lost, preach the gospel, save souls, and build the kingdom of God on earth through our good deeds. That is what the power of God is about. It is not to make pastors rich or for churches to demonstrate how wealthy they can be. It is not for the pyrotechnics of the Holy Spirit. It is to demonstrate the love of God for all humanity so that the lost can see and be saved. Until the Church turns toward Jerusalem and reconnects with its history and its roots, it will not be able to restore the power or the love or the relationship that it has with God.

Reconnecting to our roots means coming to grips with the importance of the Torah and the Old Testament in general for our daily lives. Far too many well-meaning but mistaken Christians say, "Don't you know that the Old Testament and the Torah are finished and that we don't need it anymore? Don't you know that we are free from the Law?" Freedom is not supposed to bring anarchy or a lack of rules and standards in one's life, however. The truth is that one cannot be free from something he never had and that he has despised all his life. What I would say to all these people is to first of all, get into it and see what it is before judging it. *"Taste and see that the Lord is good,"* Psalm 34:9 says.

I would like to offer a challenge to all my Jewish and Christian friends reading these words: try keeping the Sabbath for a while and see if it helps and blesses your life. Yeshua is the Lord of the Sabbath. How could He be Lord of something that is bad or that we do not need? Yeshua is Lord of the Sabbath because there is value to the Sabbath. The Church says, "We don't need the Sabbath because we have Sunday," but they are only deceiving and injuring themselves. The families of the West are the biggest victims of this modern lifestyle, which has destroyed the very fiber of the American family. One of the reasons is because they do not observe a Sabbath, and the Sabbath is like every other day for them. If people stayed at home with their wives, children, and grandchildren and did not go shopping or to work and had dinner together on Friday night as a family at least one day a week, then they would taste the wisdom of God in saying, "Work six days and rest on the seventh."

The Catholic Church purposefully changed the Sabbath to Sunday in the Fifth Century, and there is no place in the Bible that says to rest on Sunday or that Sunday is the Christian Sabbath. The Church made a bad interpretation of some of the practices in the New Testament and changed the Sabbath into Sunday based on their poor interpretations. According to Acts 20:7, the Church met on the first day of the week, immediately after the Sabbath, on Saturday night, as the Greek says literally. That was when the early Church met to worship, but it did not replace the day of rest when God rested. The Church in Rome replaced the Sabbath and strayed from the New Testament in many other ways, too. That is why we have to resolutely turn our faces to Jerusalem like Yeshua did.

I was raised as a Jewish kid in Jerusalem without a lot of religion. My parents were atheists, and I knew very little about Judaism and absolutely nothing about Christianity. I had never spoken to a Christian in my life, and I was very fortunate that I got to know Yeshua before I got to know Christianity. If I had known anything about Christianity before I knew Yeshua, I would never have believed in Him.

A high school teacher once asked me to write a paper about the beginning of Christianity for a history class. He told me to start by reading a Hebrew encyclopedia about Christianity and to go on from there. I read in that encyclopedia that Christianity is divided into two major halves, Catholic and Protestant. I read that Christianity's major holidays are Christmas, Easter, Halloween, St. Valentine's Day, etc. I read that the Protestants are divided into two halves as well, the Arminians and the Calvinists. The bibliography of this encyclopedia listed the New Testament, and when I read the chapters my high school teacher assigned to me, I got very upset because I could not find anything "Christian" (according to the definition of Christianity in the encyclopedia) in the New Testament.

I looked for "Protestants," but the only "Protestants" I saw were the Pharisees, who were protesting against Yeshua. I looked for Christian holidays but did not find any of them in the New Testament. All I found was a story about a Jewish boy who was born in Bethlehem, just six miles from where I lived. I found someone who dealt with problems that occupied me as a Jewish boy, like my attitude toward the Sabbath and the religious establishment and the hypocrisy of the religious people in my neighborhood. I did not find a single Christian thing in the New Testament; it was all Jewish. I looked for the Baptists and only found one Baptist, who also happened to be a Jew. That is what intrigued me as a Jewish boy in Jerusalem and caused me to dig more deeply into the Word of God and to find out who this Yeshua really was.

I made my decision after two years of struggling with the torment in my soul because, as a Jew, I did not want to become a Christian, but I did want to be saved. I was selfish enough to desire to be saved and ensure my eternal life, and I knew there was no other way than Yeshua the Messiah. This is my story, but my discovery of the differences between the Jewish Messiah Yeshua in the Jewish book of the New Testament and the Christianity of today should help us all see how far we have strayed off the right path and how much backtracking we need to do in order to return to the truth of God's Word.

The Church needs to stop seeking to return to the "pure truths of the Reformation." In my opinion, it is too late to reform the Church, and the Reformation made a lot of serious mistakes. Instead of reformation, we need to start seeking *restoration.* In Israel God is restoring the dry bones back to life and the Land back to its rightful owners. God is restoring the Spirit back to the Church and life back to the dead valleys of the Negev and to the Jordan Valley. The desert is blooming again, and as Israel is being restored physically, the Church needs to be restored spiritually. It will only happen as we turn our faces together back toward Jerusalem.

When I became a believer, there were many missionaries in Jerusalem: Baptists, Pentecostals, Church of Christ, etc. Each one had six or seven Jews in their congregation. The biggest congregation was about fifty people, half of whom were Jewish, but the same people in that congregation were attending all the other congregations as well because they were benefiting financially from doing so. The missionaries were helping them with clothing and other material needs because all these believers were poor. In the whole country in 1962, there were maybe only fifty Jews who believed in Yeshua.

Today it is completely different, and we have close to a hundred local congregations, which are not part of some international mission or denomination. They sing and worship in Hebrew, and most of them are seeking, to one degree or another, their roots in Judaism. They are slowly getting Torah scrolls and beginning to pray and celebrate holidays like Jews. There are thousands of Jewish believers now, and the congregations are growing. This is a miracle of restoration from God and a sign that the time is soon to come when Jerusalem will return to being the center of the Church and will be universally recognized as the center of God's plan. Christians all over the world have begun "back to Jerusalem" movements and are seeking the knowledge of the God of Israel and to reconnect with the Jewish people. When one looks at the tragic history of Christian persecutions of Jews, these phenomena are nothing less than miracles that mark the Restoration of Israel and the Church back to the true source.

We have realized that we are not in the process of *reformation*, but rather in the process of *restoration*. We are not looking to Europe or Rome for our inspiration, but rather are turning our faces toward Jerusalem. We should all turn our faces toward Jerusalem because the next appointment on God's calendar is going to be in Jerusalem. Yeshua is coming back to the Mount of Olives in Jerusalem, and we need to be ready for his soon return!

Chapter Six:

"Grace and Truth"

One interesting difference in mentality between most of the Western world and the Middle East relates to property. In the West people tend to try to acquire as many things as possible, even if that means that they buy many cheap versions of the same object. For example, Americans generally want to own several suits, even if they are not all high-quality, so that they can have variety and appear to own lots of property. In contrast, many of the Jews and the Arabs in the Middle East would rather have one good suit than a lot of average ones. They only want one car, but it has to be a Mercedes. They believe not in having a lot of junk, but in having the best version of the one item that is necessary. This is a marked difference in the mentality of the West and the East. People who live in tents, like the Bedouins in the desert, will still wear an *abaya*, but it is made from top-grade British wool. They leave the brand name on the edge so that everyone can see it, too. It is a part of our mentality to want the best.

In the same way we should know that as children of God, we deserve the best, and there is absolutely nothing better than the truth. The Jewish people have known this for a long time and have been willing to sacrifice their lives for the truth of God's Word and the laws of the Torah through centuries of persecution because they know how important these truths are. In their misunderstanding of true spiritual values, centuries of Western Christian theologians have declared that they do not need the treasure of the Torah anymore, but they do not know what they are missing. They mistakenly believe that the Hebrew Bible is only full of law, punishment, and judgment and that Yeshua had to come to introduce the concepts of grace, love, and mercy into the world. These beliefs could not be further from the truth, so this chapter will try to demonstrate a more accurate understanding of God's grace and truth as it appears in the entire Bible.

John 1:17 is very often used in Christian theology to justify their wrong interpretation, so we are going to examine it closely here. *"For the Law was given through Moses; grace and truth came through Yeshua the Messiah."* The meaning of this verse is not oppositional, the way many people see it at first glance. People think it implies that the Law is the opposite of grace and truth. This wrong interpretation leads people to think that before Yeshua there was no grace and truth and that before Him all we had was the Law. When Yeshua came, He brought grace and truth into the world, which had never seen these ideals before, according to this point of view.

Sharply contradicting this interpretation is the fact that this phrase "grace and truth" appears about twenty times in the Hebrew Bible. Most English Bibles do not have the phrase "grace and truth" in any other place in the New or Old Testament, though, because they choose to use other words that fit their preconceptions better. Some translations use "grace and truth" once or twice in a Messianic passage in the Old Testament, but most do not have it at all. A look at the Bible in Hebrew, however, reveals this exact phrase, "grace and truth," over and over. In most Christian Bible translations, the words *grace and truth* are replaced with synonyms like *graciousness* and *loving-kindness* instead of *grace,* and words like *faithfulness* and *truthfulness* instead of *truth.* Yet in Hebrew, it is all the same phrase, *chesed* [grace] and *emet* [truth], so we cannot say that the Torah does not have any grace and truth in it. John 1:17 is really quoting directly from the Torah when it uses this phrase and is certainly not saying that Yeshua brought grace into the world for the first time.

Another example of serious translation problems like this is the word *gospel,* or *besorah* in Hebrew. The word *gospel* is not really an English word but, in fact, is a Celtic word; and it is used only in the New Testament to translate the Greek word *evangelion* [the Good News]. In the New Testament, this word is translated into English as *gospel,* but the equivalent Hebrew word in the Old Testament (*besorah*) is translated as *Good News* or *Good Tidings* in English. This, of course, means that one will not find the word *gospel* in the Old Testament by looking in an English concordance, even though it really is present.

Returning to our original text, however, let us first analyze what John means. He says that the Law was handed down *through* Moses. Moses was not the source of the Torah; he was only an agent. He received it and handed it down. It came through him, but it was not his. He received it from God and gave it to the people at Mt. Sinai as a sort of mediator between them and God. On the other hand, *"Grace and truth came through Yeshua the Messiah"* who was not only an agent like Moses, but also the holy source of these ideals, even in the Hebrew Bible.

It is hard to understand this text without looking at the general context, which is revealed in verse 18. *"No one has ever seen God, but the only begotten Son, who is at the Father's side, has made him known."* The context deals with the issue of seeing God, and the text says that no one has ever seen God except the Son. There are many obscure statements connected with this idea of seeing God in the rest of John's first chapter, where it talks about Yeshua being the Light that *shone in the darkness*. It also has statements like *No one has seen Him* and *He brought grace upon grace*. If checked carefully with a Bible and a concordance, all these phrases lead to one passage in the Torah, which is their source.

Before we look into that, though, let us check our understanding of the words *grace* and *truth*. They are actually two mutually exclusive things. Grace does not go with truth and vice versa. If I go to the grocery store to buy a pound of beef, and the butcher weighs exactly a pound of beef, he is giving me the true weight of what I bought. If I want the true weight of what I paid for, it will be exactly one pound. If he gives me a pound and a quarter, though, and does not charge me extra, it is no longer truth, but instead has turned into grace. If we rely on grace, it means we are relying on something that is above and beyond the truth.

According to the truth of God's standards of justice, we are guilty and ought to go to hell, but according to grace, we are free. If we are measured by the truth, we will be in the same situation as the Psalmist who said in Psalm 130:3, *"If you, O Lord, kept a record of sins, O Lord, who could stand?"* We are all sinners compared to the true standards of God. When grace enters, it transforms the truth and produces through the love of God a freedom from sin that is above and beyond the true measure of what we really deserve. Grace tears up the evil decree of judgment against us that we deserve for our sins. When John says that *"Grace and truth came through Yeshua the Messiah,"* he means that these two conflicting elements have been joined in this one person, Yeshua the Messiah.

We can also see these principles at work in Proverbs 16:6, *"By **grace** [chesed] and **truth** [emet] iniquity will be atoned for, and by the fear of the Lord one turns away from evil."* This verse provides a very interesting background to the idea of Yeshua, the epitome of grace and truth, bringing atonement for our sins, just as John says. Let us also quickly review a couple of other occurrences of this phrase in the Hebrew Bible to get a better idea of what it means.

The first place the phrase *grace and truth* appears in the Bible is in the very interesting context of the story of when Abraham sent Eleazar back to his family in Haran to find and bring back a bride for his son Isaac. He sent him to his brother-in-law Laban, who was not a very honest person. Laban saw that Eleazar brought a lot of gold and gifts for the bride but that Eleazar had not given all the gifts yet, so he wanted to keep Rebecca a little bit longer until he got it all. Then Eleazar told Laban in Genesis 24:49, *"Now if you will show **grace and truth** [chesed v'emet] to my master, tell me; and if not, tell me, so I may know which way to turn."* He wanted to know whether to stay or to go, whether to close the deal or to cancel it. Eleazar asked Laban to be fair and truthful with him and to lay the cards on the table for him so that he would know where he stood. He also wanted Laban to do the loving thing for his relative and send Rebecca to be Isaac's bride.

This same phrase is used again in Genesis 47:29-30: *"When the time drew near for Israel to die, he called for his son Joseph and said to him, 'If I have found favor in your eyes, put your hand under my thigh and promise that you will show me **grace and truth** [chesed v'emet]. Do not bury me in Egypt, but when I rest with my fathers, carry me out of Egypt and bury me where they are buried.' 'I will do as you say,' Joseph said."* Jacob asked Joseph to show him grace and truth and not to leave him buried in Egypt, but to take him to Hebron, where Abraham and Isaac are buried, in the land of God's promise to the children of Israel.

The most important passage from the Torah that contains grace and truth, however, occurs in Exodus 33-34, which is John's source for these statements in his prologue. Exodus 33 speaks about Moses' second encounter with God after the destruction of the golden calf. The first time that Moses went up to the mountain and stayed forty days, the children of Israel sinned and built the golden calf with Aaron and worshipped it. When Moses came down the mountain with the Ten Commandments, he got so angry at what he saw and heard – with the wild dancing, singing, eating, and carousing in front of the golden calf – that he broke the tablets of the Ten Commandments.

After this incident Exodus 33 then describes what happened the second time Moses climbed the mountain. God first declared that He would send an angel with Israel to lead them into the Promised Land, instead of going with them Himself, because He was afraid He would not be able to bear their sin any longer and would consume them in his anger. Moses did not like this idea at all, however, and so he began to argue with the Lord. Exodus 33:12-13 continues the account, *"Moses said to the Lord, 'You have been telling me: "Lead these people," but you have not let me know whom you will send with me. You have said, "I know you by name, and you have found favor with me." If you are pleased with me, teach me your ways so that I may know you and continue to find favor with you. Remember that this nation is your people.'"*

God told Moses to lead the people, but Moses told Him, "I cannot do it unless I get to know You on a more personal basis. I need to establish a close relationship and be able to communicate with You, or else I cannot lead this people because they are Your people. They are not my people; they are Your children. In order for me to be able to do a good job leading these people, I have to get to know You more." Moses did not want a mere angel to accompany them, but God Himself. He knew he needed all the help he could get in order to lead his people properly. This need for the help of the presence of God is true for every leader in God's church. Apparently Moses' words were convincing because verse 14 says, *"The Lord replied, 'My Presence will go with you, and I will give you rest.'"*

As any spiritual leader knows, trying to lead people on the path to God is exhausting work that never seems to cease or allow any time for rest. When we try to do all this work on our own and do not rely on the help of the Lord, we get physical and spiritual burn-out. We humans try to do a whole lot of things on our own, but there always comes a breaking point at which we cannot manage on our own any longer. The task of the Presence of the Lord, the *Shechinah,* as Rabbinic Hebrew began to call it, is to accompany us and give us rest. God said to Moses, "If you want to know me better and have a personal relationship with Me, I will send you My Presence to give you rest from leading this enormous rabble of slaves to freedom." Moses was not satisfied with this promise alone, however, and insisted on clarifying matters.

Verse 15 says, *"Then Moses said to him, 'If your Presence does not go with us, do not send us up from here.'"* In other words, "We are going nowhere unless You give us the *Shechinah* and Your Presence. We will just stay right here." Then he continues in verse 16, *"How will anyone know that you are pleased with me and with your people unless you go with us? What else will distinguish me and your people from all the other people on the face of the earth?"*

What a statement that is! What else will distinguish God's people from all the other people on the face of the earth if it is not the Presence of the Lord with us where we are? The Presence of God accompanying us will distinguish us from all the other people in the world! As individual husbands, wives, children, and leaders, we need that Presence because we want to be distinguished from the world. We do not want to fall into the trap of the fake Hollywood existence that the world is handing down to us. We need the world to see God's blessing in our lives as his Spirit lives within us and helps us, both in the good times and the bad times. Seeing God's Spirit within us as we go through our lives is what attracts the lost to the hope of the Messiah that we carry. We do not need to present a façade of being unshakable on our own power; but when people see God helping us through our difficulties, it is a powerful witness.

In response verses 17-18 say, *"And the Lord said to Moses, 'I will do the very thing you have asked because I am pleased with you, and I know you by name.' Then Moses said, 'Now show me your glory.'"*

Notice how Moses was bargaining with God. When God gave him a little, he asked for just a little bit more. As children of God, we all have to understand God and how He works. He is like a good, loving father, but He does not give everything to his children on a silver platter immediately because if He does, they will never appreciate it. He likes it when we ask Him for the things we need and desire. Therefore, as we see in this passage, God said, "All right, Moses, I'll give you what you want." Yet Moses answered, "Wait a minute, what I really want is to see Your glory!" We might see this statement as being a little presumptuous and the whole concept of arguing with God this way as problematic, but the text does not blame Moses at all for what he said or did here.

Exodus 33:19-20 continues this conversation with a beautiful act of the Lord. *"And the Lord said, 'I will cause all my goodness to pass in front of you, and I will proclaim my name, the Lord, in your presence. I will have mercy on whom I will have mercy, and I will have compassion on whom I will have compassion. But,' he said, 'you cannot see my face, for no one may see me and live.'"* Moses wanted to see God's glory, and God answered him, "I'll do everything I can to show you My goodness, but you should know that no man can see My face and live. I'll show you My goodness, but no man can see My face." God is so holy that we as sinful people cannot see Him and live. His power and glory are so overwhelming that in our current state, we could not possibly bear to see them in their fullness. Often in the Bible the phrase "lift up one's face" or "show one's face" means to show mercy, goodness, and favor and has nothing to do with physically seeing a face. God's goodness is so overwhelmingly powerful, however, that humans on this earth cannot survive seeing the depth of his goodness. When the Messiah returns though, we will be able to see and comprehend his plan and his goodness in full, as 1 Corinthians 13:12 says, "Now we see in a glass darkly; then we shall see face to face. Now I know in part; then I shall know fully, even as I am fully known."

Verses 21-23 continue: *"Then the Lord said, 'There is a place near me where you may stand on a rock. When my glory passes by, I will put you in a cleft in the rock and cover you with my hand until I have passed by. Then I will remove my hand, and you will see my back; but my face must not be seen.'"* God told Moses, "I will show you My back but not My face. Stand on that rock over there, and I will hide you from My Presence with My own hand. Then after I pass by, I will remove My hand, and you will see My back." Moses climbed onto a rock, and the Lord came down. Even seeing God's back was probably a very overwhelming experience, despite the fact that Moses was used to speaking with God and being in his Presence all the time.

The most beautiful part of Moses' seeing God's Presence appears in what the Lord said to him as He passed by. Exodus 34:5-7 recounts, *"Then the Lord came down in a cloud and stood there with him and proclaimed his name, the Lord. And he passed in front of Moses, proclaiming, 'The Lord, the Lord, the compassionate and gracious God, slow to anger, abounding in* **grace** *[chesed] and* **truth** *[emet]. Keeping* **grace** *[chesed] to thousands, and forgiving wickedness, rebellion, and sin. Yet he does not leave the guilty unpunished; he punishes the children and their children for the sins of their fathers to the third and fourth generation.'"*

Now we have grace and truth in this passage from the Torah, and verse 7 tells us that there is another grace, which is kept in storage for the future. The Hebrew word for *keeping* here speaks about a future grace that will be preserved for the multitude of thousands, for the forgiveness of their sins, and for their atonement. There are two kinds of grace here then. There is **grace and truth** apparent already in God's relationship with Israel in the Torah and the **preserved grace** that is for the many, for the forgiveness of sins of the whole world. This passage is the source of what John is talking about. When John says that no one has seen God, it is clear that he took the idea from this text in Exodus. *"Grace and truth came through Yeshua the Messiah"* is directly taken from this passage in the Torah, which talks about the grace and truth of God in his relationship with Israel.

The Jews say that there are thirteen characteristics in the nature of God, and they are all taken from this text. *"The Lord, the Lord, the compassionate and gracious God, slow to anger, abounding in grace* [chesed] *and truth* [emet], *preserving grace* [chesed] *for the thousands, and forgiving wickedness, rebellion, and sin."* That is the very essence of the character of God. Two of these characteristics are God's grace and truth, and only in the Messiah can we find these characteristics standing together without conflict on this earth. He was the truth because He gave his life, and He was the grace because through Him, grace has come to the thousands, to the many. That preserved grace of God, about which Exodus 34:7 speaks, and the original grace of God, which is in the Torah, are put together when John 1:16 says, *"In him we have received grace upon grace."* The two kinds of grace, one from the Torah and one from the cross, are characterized in the character, nature, mission, and person of Yeshua the Messiah.

The Law was given through Moses; Moses was the agent through whom the Law was handed down to the people. Nevertheless, the essence and the very purpose of the Torah were accomplished by Yeshua the Messiah. He was the embodiment of the Torah in the person of the Messiah. He became our living Torah; and through Him, we can enjoy the Torah without the burden and curse of the punishments we deserve for our sin, without the guilt that comes from our own weakness, and without the condemnation that comes from our sins. He became the true essence and fulfillment of the Torah by living a completely perfect life but still paying the price of the just punishments God prescribed in the Torah for the violation of his standards. He fulfilled all the positive and negative requirements of the Torah in his life and death for our sakes.

The Book of Hebrews teaches this idea extensively, but here in the Gospel of John, we are told that the very essence of the character of God, which was promised in the Torah, was accomplished by Yeshua the Messiah. No man has seen the Lord, but the Son has seen Him and has revealed the Father to us. Another text in John 14:9 says, *"Whoever has seen the Son has also seen the Father"* because He is the embodiment of the Father in the flesh down here on earth. He did not come to cancel or destroy the Torah; He came to fulfill the Torah by becoming the grace and truth of God in one person.

We see, therefore, that in the Messiah Yeshua, these two conflicting elements become a part of the very nature of what Yeshua did. What God did in sending his beloved Son to die for a bunch of rebellious people who hated God was horrible, at least from a certain type of perspective. He sacrificed his Son as the ultimate payment for unrighteousness and sin. This was the ultimate righteous act, the ultimate truth, to pay for the wrong that humanity had done. Yet that same act that was so gruesome and so horrible was also a demonstration of the great love and grace of God. As human beings, we have a hard time understanding and appreciating this because we are on this side of the veil. We cannot understand it until we experience something of it ourselves.

One of the most famous kidney doctors in Japan told the following story that beautifully illustrates grace and truth of this variety. He came from a poor family with one son and four daughters. The father of the family did not send the daughters to school because, before World War II, it was not fashionable to send women to high school and university or to let them become professionals. The girls worked as house cleaners, in retail, and all kinds of other menial jobs, while the father took their money to send his son to medical school. Finally, the son went to America and became a specialist in kidney transplants, but the girls felt a little bit used and neglected as a result of this.

They felt that an injustice had been done to them because they did not go to school, and their money only went to send their brother to school. When their brother returned to Japan, he became a very wealthy and famous doctor, one of the leading kidney transplant doctors in Japan. Yet, understandably, the girls always harbored a bitter streak and a bit of anger about what their father had done. They could not go to school, and their money was taken from them to be given to this boy to go to school instead.

Eventually, one of the girls became ill, and her kidneys stopped functioning. Her brother operated on her to give her a kidney transplant, but her body would not accept the kidney. She was going to die, and there was nothing she could do about it. Then she was invited to come back to the hospital for a second kidney transplant. Completely unexpectedly, when she woke up from the surgery, she saw that her brother was in the bed next to her. He had given her one of his kidneys, which gave her another chance at life. At that moment, she suddenly understood that the sacrifice her father had forced the sisters to make had paid off in the end and saved her life, whether it fit the earthly standards of justice or not.

We can all understand this story, but God did it on a mega-scale for all of humanity. God did it for each one of us! He laid down his Son's life and gave the life of the Messiah Himself for our transgressions, so that by his stripes we may be healed and so that by his death we may gain life. In Him the very essence of what the Torah is all about is concentrated. The Torah came through Moses, but the essence of the Torah, the grace and truth of God, was revealed to the world through Yeshua the Messiah who satisfied the standards of truth for us and gave us grace.

John 1:17 is not saying that there is no grace in the Torah or trying to put the Torah and grace in opposition to one other. Anyone who thinks that there is no grace in the Torah has been seriously deceived. John's prologue is based on what happened on Mt. Sinai between God and Moses. John tells us that what Moses wanted to see, the very glory of God, was revealed to us in Yeshua. Yeshua is the revelation of God's glory; He is the face of God in the flesh. He is the Jewish Messiah for which Israel has waited, missed the first time, and will accept the second time without a shadow of a doubt because God promised, "All Israel shall be saved!" Non-Jewish believers are also a part of that great promise and have been grafted into that natural olive tree to become a part of the people of Israel, not replacing them, but joining with them into the inheritance of Abraham.

In order to get the full picture and see the whole revelation, the Church has to reconnect with Israel. There cannot be a New Testament Church without Jews because the Church which God is building is formed from the two peoples that become one. The Church is made up of Jews and Gentiles of all colors and ethnicities. A Church without Jews in it is like a soup without salt or a kitchen without a knife.

God designed the Church to be inseparably connected with Jerusalem and the Torah. He did not make it to be **under** the Torah because being **under** the Torah is a bad thing. The phrase "to be under" is taken from the Torah's commandment about helping one's enemy's donkey in Exodus 23:5, which says, *"If you see your enemy's donkey fallen down under burden, you shall refrain from leaving him with it; you shall rescue it with him."* This verse says that when we see our neighbor's donkey *under a burden* that is too big for it and keeps it from being able to walk, we should lift up the burden and relieve the donkey so that it can walk and do its job. We are not **under** the Torah; we are **under** God's grace. Because we are under God's grace and because we have been given the Presence of God, the *Shechinah* or the Holy Spirit, we can do God's will. We can keep his commandments because the Spirit of God leads us into all truth and enables us to do the will of God without feeling burdened by his commandments.

It is not hard to do the commandments, but it is hard to show the love that we have for God. It is much harder to show my neighbor that I love him than to keep kosher or salt my meat. It is easy to get used to the physical commandments of God, but what is hard is to have the attitudes, the spirit, and the love that we are commanded to have toward one another. The Holy Spirit is given to us, just as it was given to Moses in the text we read above, to help us fulfill God's purposes for our lives. The Presence of God enabled Moses to lead the people and to feel that he was not alone, which granted him rest. God told him that He would give Moses his Presence so that Moses could rest, and He does the same for us too. God does not want us to be like that donkey; He wants us to find rest in Him. We will find rest because the Lord of the Sabbath is also our Lord, and He promised, *"Come unto me, all you that are weary and heavy burdened, and I will give you rest. Take my yoke upon you and learn from me, for I am gentle and lowly in heart, and you will find rest for your souls. For my yoke is easy, and my burden is light."[1]* His Spirit within us is what allows us to fulfill the commandments of God without them becoming a heavy burden.

Everything that is promised in the Bible is based on reality, and God has demonstrated that reality through the Jewish people around the world. For two thousand years and more,

---

1   Matthew 11:28-30

the world has looked at the Jews and said, "These people have no nation and will never have a nation. They will never have anything or amount to anything. They will always be wandering Jews and a cursed nation." Nevertheless, we have arisen from the ashes of the Holocaust and demonstrated to the world that God is keeping his promises even in our own times. He will continue keeping his promises to Israel, to the Church, to each one of us, and to humanity. We just have to taste God and see that He is good! His *grace and truth* have touched our lives and will continue to renew us from the inside out as we allow Him to work in us.